Brighton Quakers
1655–2005

Richard S. Harrison

GW00503917

The Religious Society of Friends
Brighton Meeting

Published by Brighton Preparative Meeting, The Religious Society of Friends
Copyright © Richard S. Harrison 2005
First published 2005

ISBN 0 904733 23 8

Preface

Q UAKERS might express their individual views in different ways, but, like the spokes of the wheel, starting from different points, are focused ultimately on the one centre. The first Quakers valued the words of the Bible, but even more, they valued the illumined and transformed heart. Quakerism does not rest on creed or dogma and, as promoted by George Fox in the mid-seventeenth century, is a presentation of the original Gospel that the historical Jesus lived in flesh and blood. Quakerism, in the words of the Quaker Carl Heath (1869-1950), is

> a religion rooted in a personal and communal relationship, a progressive understanding and a creative love, an all-round intensification of personality ... a doctrine of God with us; the Spirit radiant on the face of Christ and deep in the very structure of the souls of all men. It has no finality, for it rests upon developing experience ... the testimony of the Holy Spirit, the daily witness to love and knowledge in the soul of man.

Implicit in the inspired individualism of George Fox was, and remains, the communal miracle of Quaker worship. Week by week, in their silent meetings for worship Quakers seek to be open to the presence of God. In the concentrated, attentive silences of their meetings someone, anyone, might feel an internal and spiritual prompting to speak, to share a thought, an experience, a reading, a prayer. The words, short, simple and from the heart, are not the aim of the meeting but merely contribute to deepen the worship and sense of adoration, refreshing the spirit and leaving the participants better equipped to face the challenges of life in the forthcoming week.

For 350 years Brighton's Quakers have faithfully witnessed to the message first brought to the town by inspired and caring men and women. The best evidence of their motivation or belief is to be found in their own words, as well as in what they did to help their neighbours in every way possible. For that reason this little book has not attempted any big statements of belief, about which much has been written, but has simply recorded details and stories about the Quakers who lived and worked in Brighton in the not-so-long-ago. Aware of inadequacies in my account, it remains, nevertheless, a token of my gratefulness to the Brighton Quaker Meeting, where I first joined the Religious Society of Friends and was privileged to meet many of the 'old stock', and heard from them 'the words of life'.

A Brief Note on Particular Usages

THROUGHOUT this book, in keeping with established practice, I have used the words 'Quaker' and 'Friend' synonymously to refer to members of the Religious Society of Friends. Here, also, following the convention in Quaker historical writing, dates have been left in the form ('Plain Language') in which they are found. This facilitates retrieval and is true to the insight of the original Quakers who, using biblical precedent, referred to days and months by number. Days were, and among some Friends still are, called First-day (Sunday), Second-day (Monday) and so on. Before 1752, when the Julian Calendar was instituted, First-month was applied to the month called March, Second-month to April, etc. When the 'New Style' calendar came in, First-month was then applied to the month called by non-Quakers January, the rest of the months following in numerical sequence.

Another feature of 'Plain Language' involved maintaining the older and sometimes dialect grammatical form of 'thou' and 'thee' to refer to an individual and to the Deity, and 'you' and 'ye' to refer to several people. In terms of seventeenth-century convention this Quaker usage asserted an egalitarian viewpoint and avoided giving false respect to individuals. It was, further, scriptural, following the King James Bible, and pointed to something about the 'otherness' and the uniqueness of the Deity. Strangely, Quakers, somewhat ungrammatically, sometimes dropped 'thou' and said 'thee' in all cases of the second person singular!

Thanks

I THANK in particular the staff of the East Sussex Record Office, who have assisted me in my access to documents and also the staff of Hove Library and Brighton Public Library and local history centre, as well as the Curator of the Booth Museum. Josef Keith of the Friends Historical Library, London, facilitated my work and Leslie Fuhrman also went the extra mile and kindly let me look at some of the records held at Ship Street. John Patching was most helpful to me, sharing copies of material about his family, and I have appreciated and enjoyed working with the Brighton Bicentenary Committee. My dear Friend Patricia Norman has indeed been both Martha and Mary to me, and I owe numerous debts of gratitude to Brighton Friends generally, not least to those who were there for me and encouraged me to join in the first place. Grateful thanks are also due to all those members of Brighton Meeting, past and present, who have shared their memories so generously. To Peter W. Lamb and David G. Bass, the Cork Monthly Meeting Library, and Muriel Green of the Lisburn Quaker Archives I express my thanks for photographs, access to books and other assistance.

Thanks are also due to QueenSpark Books for their assistance with the ISBN registration and distribution. www.queensparkbooks.org.uk

Richard S. Harrison

1.
THE QUAKERS OF BRIGHTHELMSTON 1655–99

'Mud and filth were thrown into the house'

SOMETHING has already been said about Quaker beliefs, but, in a seventeenth-century world of political, spiritual and social turmoil, not unlike our own, one Nicholas Beard of Rottingdean was the first Quaker to emerge in the vicinity of Brighton. A 'tender, seeking young man' he sometimes rode for twenty or thirty miles hoping to hear the words of life. The teachings of George Fox, founder of the Friends movement, were a huge influence on Beard, and in 1655 he decided to join the Quakers. He then travelled widely in Sussex and the neighbouring counties to preach the good news. His beliefs proved costly, since Quakers would not pay church dues, or bear arms or join the militia, and were often, therefore, at the receiving end of fierce persecution. Nicholas Beard was imprisoned at Lewes, and distrained of property to the value of £1,000, which would have been a huge sum in those days. But he was constant in his faith, sound in doctrine and fervent in prayer, often remarking to his children, 'That which is right do, and the Lord be with you.' At other times, having a sense of the Lord's goodness, he would say, 'Be thou bowed before the Lord, Oh! My soul.'

The new Quaker community had practical needs and looked after each other, and even more so when they were often denied, or were unwilling to receive, support from the parish. They organised an administration of their own to keep records and registers, to list births, marriages and deaths. A separate birth-register for the district near Brighton was started in 1656, and Richard Webb of 'Mouscombe near Patcham', and Richard Beard of Rottingdean, are noted among the parents. Quaker meetings for worship were held in Rottingdean in private houses, and the first burial ground was there also, on lands called Challoners, 'bounded west by the Common or Green'. The first burial there was recorded in 1659, and the ground was bought by Nicholas Beard from a Thomas Alberton in 1661. In 1675 it was leased for £20 to the Quakers for 999 years.

The first Quaker meeting for worship in Brighton is recorded for 1658, at 'the house of William Gold'. While the meeting was taking place, the other citizens of the town were streaming out of their own places of worship. Being well fortified with the doctrines of love and forgiveness, they attacked the Quakers assembled within. Mud and filth were thrown into the house, and the Quakers hauled out and threatened that they would be thrown into the sea. One attacking lady was so devout that she used her Bible to break the windows of the house. It is reported that Margery Caustock and her daughter were much abused, and one of them lost an eye when stones were thrown at her. There was real cause for fear as another Brighton Quaker, Richard Pratt, had some time before been killed by stones thrown at him. When a John Pullot dared to address the priest and the people in the 'steeple-house', which is what Quakers called churches, he was sentenced to six months' hard labour. The steeple-house in Brighton was likely to have been St Nicholas's on the Dyke Road. Persecution did not discourage these new believers, however, and when in 1659 Nicholas Beard went on a similar mission to the various steeple-houses, he was not expecting a welcome. On one occasion his hearers pulled him out by the hair of his head, and even the priest lent a hand.

Persecution reached such a high point that one young Quaker, Thomas Carver, determined to do something about it. His qualifications for the task were good; he was descended from Brighton man Deryck Carver, who once owned the Black Lion public house, and who was martyred for his religious beliefs. Thomas Carver had been one of the crew of the boat *Surprise*, which, in 1651, had taken King Charles II to safety in France. By 1669, the King had returned to his throne, and Carver, who had carried him through the waves and into the rescue boat, decided it was high time to remind Charles about it. He approached the King, who at first thought him a mere self-seeker, but was surprised to discover that he only wanted liberty for the imprisoned Quakers. The King offered to free six Quakers, and Carver retorted, 'Is that all a King's life is worth?' The bold reply seized the King's attention so much, it is supposed, that the Quakers were all freed soon after.

The owner of the *Surprise*, Nicholas Tettersall, was of a more mercenary mind, and had demanded £60 from the King for his services. Later, he became a prime persecutor of Quakers, especially in Brighton in 1670 when he was the High Constable of the town. The historian John G. Bishop notes of Tettersall that he operated 'with the zeal of a bigot and the malign industry of a ministerial spy'. When Quaker meetings were prohibited by statute, he claimed he heard a voice elevated in prayer in the house of William Beard. Having obtained a warrant and broken down the door Beard was arrested and fined £20. Quakers, however, always insisted on holding their meetings publicly, and disdained to meet behind locked doors.

An increasing number of Quaker adherents encouraged the setting up of a wider Quaker organisational structure, which included Brighton in the Lewes 'Monthly Meeting'. Monthly Meeting met at different local venues and Quakers from various places round about came together to discuss the affairs of the church. It was first held on 2 Ninth-month 1668, at Blatchington House, the residence of the widow Scrase in West Blatchington, and next on the 17 Fifth-month 1669, at Henry Scrase's house. Apart from meetings for worship held in houses owned by the Scrases, meetings were, in 1678, also being held in Brighton at the houses of John Pearce and of William Beard. The first 'Monthly Meeting' held in the town was on 17 Tenth-month 1679. This was the same year that William Beard of Brighton, son of Nicholas Beard of Rottingdean, refused to pay the shilling demanded for the upkeep of the local church and was prosecuted in the Ecclesiastical Court by Henry Snook, priest of Brighthelmstone [St Nicholas] and excommunicated, although he probably did not care about that.

2.
THE TOWN ON THE CLIFF
1700–99

'By assistance of our inward Guide'

THERE are continuing records of Quaker meetings for worship taking place in and about Brighton but clearly the community needed a proper building, and in 1700 a converted malthouse was leased for 1,000 years for £105. This was in North Street and the vendor was Thomas Parsons of Cowfold, who, probably acting on behalf of the Quakers, had bought it on 31 August 1700 from Thomas and Anne Beard of Denton. The premises and attached land comprised the tenement, malthouse, outhouses and a croft of pastureland then occupied by Richard Parker. References to the property and land are found as far back as 1637 and help to fill in our picture of early Brighton. The meadowland behind the meeting-house was let and known thereafter as Quakers' Croft, and a smaller piece at the Spring Walks (Church Street) was used as a burying ground.

It must have been a matter of poignancy to the Brighton Quakers as their earliest leaders died, including, in 1702, Nicholas Beard of Rottingdean, who was eighty years old. In spite of long periods of suffering and imprisonment, and the distraint of his goods, Nicholas Beard raised a big family and left them a much-improved farm and a tidy amount of money – and, even more, the example of a conscientious life faithfully led. By his will of 1702, he bequeathed his estate to his fifteenth son and twentieth child, Daniel, and required him to 'entertain Friends in Truth and lett them have meetings in my house as freely as in my life time to seeke and worship God'. He commended his children to 'the teachings of the Lord, and the Lord in mercy be with you'.

The Scrases of West Blatchington had played a central role in the establishment of the Quaker community in Brighton. Perhaps their situation, slightly outside the town, provided a more sheltered environment in times of persecution. Walter Scrase of Preston, formerly of West Blatchington, had joined Quakers in those earlier times. He died in 1718, and in his will of that year, proved at Lewes, he was described as 'aged and infirme', and that he wished to be buried 'in the burying place of the people called Quakers, in Rottingdeane, near his relations who lye buried there'. He gave an annuity to Barbara, daughter of John Gold of Bazedean (Balsdeane) and to his kinsman Charles Scrase, 'late of Blatchington, now of Brighton', he gave lands 'at Blatchingtton called Luknes Croft and his messuage and tenement' at Preston.

Living near to the Scrases at West Blatchington were the Gold and Harrison families. William Harrison (d.1680) was a shoemaker. His son, also William Harrison (c.1667–1733), at some point in his career, perhaps in the early eighteenth century, happened to be walking across Emsworth Common, near Chichester. A man came up behind him with a horse and asked him to hold it for a while, which William, being a decent obliging man, did. The horse was loaded with goods, which may have intrigued him for a while. Not long after, up galloped a troop of sweating and angry men who arrested William on the spot for the robbery of the horse and the goods. The sentence for the offence was a capital one and William Harrison's case was bleak in the extreme. After being sentenced to death, he was in chains at an inn, and, looking out of the window, he saw a man in the street below loading a dung-cart, who he recognised. William got permission to invite the man up for a glass of 'canary' wine, and when the two men met in the room, his guest nonchalantly admitted that he had indeed asked William to hold the stolen horse. He said he fully intended to take his proper place at the end of the ladder before the innocent William arrived there but had, not unnaturally, felt a little nervous about the prospect, and so had delayed confessing. The confession made and, most importantly, overheard, the thief exchanged places with William. So perhaps it might not be wise to look after someone's luggage if you are ever asked.

A degree of official and popular tolerance was eventually achieved and the pioneering Quakers were succeeded by sons and daughters of equal character to themselves. One notable figure was John Grover (1677–1752), originally of Hurstpierpoint. A shepherd, he was employed by the Scrase family of West Blatchington. In 1697, he married Elizabeth Harrison whose brother was the innocent William Harrison who was nearly hanged by mistake.

John Grover was later employed in a brewery and must have learned the brewery trade there as he is later called a maltster. Whenever he had time, he would write out mathematical problems with a piece of chalk on his shovel – perhaps the sort of wooden shovel which was used to stir the barley while it was being malted. In this way he calculated the motion of the tides and the stars, and was clearly engaged in a process of self-education, showing a genius for mathematics.

John Grover's useful qualities and remarkable abilities were recognised by the Reverend Falkner, sometime 'vicar of Brighton', who appointed him master of the Brighton Charity School. This in itself was remarkable, when it is considered that the school was run by the self-same church that had persecuted the early Quakers. John Grover did very well for himself and, using his mathematical skills and teaching abilities, soon progressed to starting his own boarding school. Being much trusted, he drew up wills and gave legal advice to his neighbours. His commercial abilities found an outlet also in the extensive purchase of property, which was the safest place to put savings. Before 1702, he lived with his family at North Street, but then moved to the East Cliff, remaining there until 1710 when he took up residence at Ship Street. When John Grover died he left a notebook of mathematical problems and rules for his children, which is described as 'supplemented by wonderful flourishes, emblematical devices of swans, fishes and other objects and gaily coloured borders and interlining'.

Details about the trades and work of these early Brighton Quakers are sparse. Records of distraints might ordinarily be reckoned as a useful source but in this case they are not available. It is just possible that, for a while, the financial penalties on Quakers in Brighton had been relaxed. The Grover family had several entrepreneurial interests. Elizabeth Grover (1706–27), daughter of John and Elizabeth Grover, was, like her father a schoolteacher, and began teaching at 'the new Schooll house' in Eleventh-month 1725[/6]. She kept a useful diary, which mentions many of the climatic mishaps of wind or rain and tide that affected Brighton. The diary also gives an idea of some of the trades other Quakers were engaged in, and mentions a boat built for her brother John. He voyaged to Stockholm, to Oporto and to the Canaries. Products such as wine, wood and iron are likely to have been traded, and Brighton was a centre for fishing on a quite considerable scale. However the town was disadvantaged by it having no natural harbour. On one occasion in 1723, Elizabeth Grover mentions a boat carrying salt to Portsmouth that had been wrecked near Brighton.

Most of the Brighton of 1744 was 'on the Cliff', and the town was built simply around North Street, East Street and West Street with a few intervening streets. To the south most of the old town below the Cliff had been swallowed up by the sea. Farming and fishing were the mainstays of the town, which blended into a pattern of gardens and fields moulded by the Downs. The town's population was in the region of 1,600 people but few of the citizens were very wealthy, and 336 houses were exempted from rates, which left 118 houses as the total of rateable premises. From the rate books of 1744–6 it appears that among the major landowners of Brighton were Quaker farmers and shopkeepers. John Grover of Ship Street was assessed (at 10d in the pound) for one shilling, as was the widow Osborne. Nicholas Beard of Ship Street was assessed for three shillings.

If Quakers refused to pay the proportion of rates due to the church, they were very anxious to help their fellow Brightonians by the administration of relief to their poorer neighbours, and by serving the town's institutions. Much of this poor relief centred on the church-run vestry on which Quakers also served, if with limited capacity. William Grover (1704–68), son of John Grover and, like his father and sister Elizabeth, a schoolteacher, was one of the town's overseers of the poor, and in 1752, at a vestry meeting at the Town Hall, he was signatory to a notice encouraging people to pay the poor rates. Married to Elizabeth Ellis, daughter of Elias Ellis of Lewes, he held offices among Friends in the Monthly Meeting and was named among the trustees of several meeting-houses in Sussex.

Although there is little information about the Brighton Quakers at this time, a stray reference in the *Lewes Journal* of 18 September 1749 records a Quaker wedding in Brighton, which must indicate some life. 'On Thursday last was married at the Quakers' Meeting at Brighthelmstone, Miss Sally Snashall of Hurstpierpoint, Sussex, an agreeable young woman with a plentiful fortune, to Mr Elijah Warring, surgeon at Alton in Hampshire.' Quaintly misunderstanding Quaker ways, the report says the 'service' was performed by Mr Thompson, 'who made an eloquent and solemn discourse'. There were 'present a great many young persons of that Society; and the ceremony was accomplished with an awful and decent regularity. They afterwards went to the Old Ship where they had a very elegant entertainment.'

Like the population of the town in general, the Quaker community, finding few economic opportunities, had dwindled. Perhaps the effects of disease and the harsh weather conditions seen across Europe in the 1740s were a factor in this. When William Grover (1752–1825) the son of William and Elizabeth Grover, grew up in the Brighton of the 1750s, he could remember that there used to be only five or six Quakers gathered for worship by the fireside of the widow Wilkins. When he finished at school, he was apprenticed among Quakers in a distant town in Essex (apprenticeships were usually served in other towns, often with Quakers, where places were available. Such apprentices often settled in their adopted towns when their apprenticeships ended). He left a collection of writings about his spiritual experience, and if most of his life was spent away from home, there is a certain brightness and clarity about his prose that is evocative of Brighton sunshine and sea-breeze.

In the 1750s Brighton had only seven major streets, less than 600 houses and perhaps 2,500 inhabitants, but it already showed signs of change. The town had become a centre for invalids and was promoted by Dr Richard Russell (1687–1759), the advocate of sea-cures, who chose it as the best place for treating people and nursing them back to vigorous health. Other visitors who were not invalids but who had time and money for a holiday also helped to boost Brighton incomes. Statistical increase began to register among the Quakers too, and this encouraged the setting up of a 'Brighton Preparative Meeting'. The decision was made 20 Third-month 1769, at a 'Quarterly Meeting' at Hurstpierpoint, and its first meeting was held on 3 Ninth-month 1769. There were only three Friends present – John Snashall, John Ticehurst and John Glaisyer – who prefaced the first minute book with the following:

> The Friends now present (though but a small number) upon reading the said minute do incline and agree to constitute such a meeting hoping that by the direction and assistance of our inward guide and the

true light and blessing of Divine Providence therein to the encouraging and strengthening of one another to be faithful to our Profession and the building of each other up in the most Holy Faith so that we may walk ... in the life of our dear Lord and Saviour Jesus Christ.

The Brighton Meeting was by no means totally preoccupied with its own spiritual life. Occasionally there was a call on it to subscribe to help needy Quakers elsewhere, as in 1778 when Thomas Cruitenden, Thomas Coates, William Tuppen, Elizabeth Grover and John Glaisyer contributed to the Monthly Meeting funds subscribed 'on behalf of our suffering Friends in America'. This was a fund to help the Friends in Britain's North American colonies who, refusing to join in the armed conflict there, suffered extensive losses of property and risk to their lives.

The chief business of the Brighton Preparative Meeting was to select representatives to the Monthly Meeting, and to read and accurately answer the 'Queries'. These Queries – and 'Advices' – had been collected in manuscript to encourage individual and corporate review of the community's spiritual and moral life. The Queries were considered in quarterly batches for report to superior meetings. The Preparative Meeting also considered some small business about rents from the attached meeting-house property, and the collection of subscriptions. Women Quakers also participated and probably, as was the custom at other levels of Quaker organisation, assembled separately. Among the attendance on 10 Third-month 1780 were Tabitha Hilton, Jane Mitchell, Elizabeth Likeman, Mary Osborne, Hannah Ticehurst and Mary Mitchell.

In 1783, the Prince of Wales paid his first visit to Brighton, ostensibly for the sake of his health, and enjoyed himself so much that he decided to build his seaside palace there. At first this was modest in conception and centred on the Marine Villa on the Steine, opened in 1787, but the air of Brighton moved him to a more grandiose scheme, which, after several aesthetic evolutions, became the Royal Pavilion. This building, in a mixture of oriental styles, was probably as surprising to the Quakers as to the other native Brightonians. The world of fashion and the Court followed the Prince down and, in addition to serving the needs of invalids who came for the sea-bathing, demand for housing and lodging rapidly increased. The Quaker community was affected by this as much as their fellow townsfolk, and were exposed to people whose morals were not necessarily very high. They were also able to help provide lodgings, and the goods and provisions required by the growing population.

Brighton offered good openings for trade and apprenticeships and in spite of the inconvenience of distraints the Quakers flourished. The town supported a profitable mackerel industry and the fishermen hauled their distinctive 'hoggie' boats up on the pebbly beaches. There was a workhouse to support the destitute, and Quakers served as civic officers. Marriage certificates give indications of the trades of some of the Brighton Quakers, and many of them were incomers to the town. Thomas Coates, son of Sarah (deceased) and Henry Coates, a husbandman of Patcham, was a carpenter and he married Jane Bartholomew, daughter of James Bartholomew, a gardener, and Jane Bartholomew, deceased. Daniel Hack (d.1823) was a shopkeeper and the son of James Hack, a leather cutter of Chichester; in 1785, he married Mary Mitchell, daughter of Mary and Henry Mitchell, a yeoman of Brighton.

A membership list for 1787 indicates in the region of 45 Quakers in Brighton. The names of some of them show up also in the 1785 East Sussex Land Tax records where there are entries for the widow Glazier (Glaisyer) and for John Glazier, a baker of 16 Black Lion Street, and for the widow Hilton of West Street. Contributing to the increase in Quaker numbers was a degree of convincement, and Richard Patching and his wife Jane are noteworthy in this respect, since they came to play a big part in the Quaker meeting. Richard Patching was accepted into membership on 14 Eleventh-month 1787, when Thomas Cruttenden and Thomas Rickman reported that they had paid a religious visit to him, and were satisfied that he was 'convinced of our religious principles'. John Glaisyer and William Tuppen were appointed to convey the acceptance to Richard. Richard Patching was the founder, in 1775, of the building firm that continues to this day in Brighton.

One incomer to Brighton was Thomas Chalk, a mariner who, with his wife Ann, moved there from Folkestone. They brought with them a certificate from their home meeting stating that they were of sober and orderly life. But Thomas Chalk had not been long in Brighton when he showed clear signs of being very argumentative and abrasive, and not particularly orderly. His old meeting was still seen as having some responsibility for him and was questioned about its certificate. In 1787, Thomas and Ann Chalk were involved in dissension with a fellow member. Such disharmony was seen as a potential interference with the meeting for worship, and it was necessary to heal the breach. So it was at the Preparative Meeting of 8 Third-month 1787 when the following was minuted:

> A concern being raised in the minds of several Friends respecting a breach of unity between Thomas Chalk and wife and Jane Mitchell and family and in order that they may be reunited in true love and fellowship this meeting thinks it prudent to appoint the following Friends to visit them on the occasion and make report – Samuel West, John Glaisyer, Jane Coates with any others that are free.

Fortunately the Quakers were able to settle their differences, to the relief of the Meeting.

The wider Quaker world prompted the Lewes Monthly Meeting to consider if all members were free of connection with the then profitable slave trade; fortunately the answer in 1786, and in other years, proved to be 'yes'. Quaker anti-slavery activity was to remain a constant. Reflecting the realities of Brighton and of Sussex, where smuggling was a very popular activity, Quakers were also asked in their 'Queries', 'Do you stand clear in our testimony against defrauding the King in his customs duties or excise, or in dealing in funds suspected to be run?' No examples of Quaker smugglers have emerged in Brighton.

Brighton Quakers, like other members of the Lewes Monthly Meeting, continued to suffer distraints of their goods for refusing to pay 'church dues' and military rates. These distraints were frequently not only for the amount demanded but also included an inflated collection charge. A shopkeeper or householder might find officials suddenly entering their premises and walking off with a set of chairs, or the goods out of the shop. These distraints were carefully listed by Friends and the Government kept informed of their grievance. The lists are of interest in showing the trades of some of the

Brighton Friends. To take some sample entries for the year 1795, John Glazier (Glaisyer) was distrained of five bushels of flour for the 'warden's rates' and the 'navy rate'. Flour was also taken from Jeremiah Prier, and Daniel Hack, a linen draper, had 25 yards of Irish linen taken from his shop. Builder William Tuppen had deals removed, and Lucy and Edward Martin lost Irish linen and eleven pair of hose.

The Chalk family continued to be a worry and when, in 1795, John Chalk, against the advice of Quakers who probably knew him better than he knew himself, entered business and went bankrupt, they were very exercised. He had not been careful in supporting his family, and his wife had been lax in its management. Attempts to meet him were frustrated by his deliberate absence, and the delegation from the Meeting had to speak to his wife instead. When she persuaded him to come in, he promptly walked out again. With evident relief, it was noted that the matter was finally 'buried in oblivion' but John Chalk did forfeit his membership. His children, however, were helped financially with their education and one of them, Thomas Chalk Jnr (d.1869), became in later years a much-respected minister among Friends.

Daniel Hack, as has been mentioned, was a linen draper of 36 East Street. He is listed as 'surveyor of the highway' and a 'collector of the highway tax' and became an important influence in Brighton. He had been widowed by this time, and was now married to Sarah Pryor (d.1817). His mother-in-law, Mary Pryor, was a recognised Quaker minister, and like many Quakers whose prayer life was deep, her spiritual antennae were definitely in 'receiving mode'. In 1797, she felt a calling to visit America and, seeking Divine Guidance, felt powerfully that she must travel in a particular ship. Her relatives, knowledgeable in business and the affairs of the sea, advised her against it and pointed out that the ship was notoriously unseaworthy. But she did as she thought right, and travelled in it anyway. Some way across the Atlantic the ship started to take on water and the passengers pumped for a week to keep it afloat. Mary Pryor told them to persevere and said she knew they would all be saved. By the second week of pumping the travellers and sailors were exhausted and just about ready to go to the bottom, and did not feel inclined to believe Mary Pryor anymore. However to cheer them up she said she knew the name of the ship that would rescue them. They, ever doubting, asked what it was, and she asked each of them to think of a surname to remind her. None seemed right, until a woman mentioned her own maiden name, and Mary Pryor said 'That is it!' and the passengers pumped away for a while longer. Sure enough, a ship soon came into view and was of the exact name that Mary Pryor had mentioned. The story did not end there. Mary Pryor's husband despaired of ever seeing her again, but his daughter told him she had dreamt that a letter from Philadelphia was on the way with the good news that his wife was safe – which is exactly what happened.

3.
REGENCY DAYS AND BEYOND
1800-46

'Very well, thank thee George!'

IN 1800, Brighton consisted of 18 streets, 1,500 houses, and upwards of 7,000 inhabitants, and was in a constant state of growth and increasing prosperity. Friends were a small but economically significant and spiritually influential group in the town. Daniel Hack, the linen draper of East Street, in 1803 was instrumental in securing the 'New Road' in place of the road that had run northwards from East Street. The exchange provided a new entrance for the Prince of Wales's palace, and thus ensured that a prime cause of the town's prosperity would not desert the place. The Prince was quite liberal in his views as well as in his morals, and got on very well in a democratic sort of a way with the Brighton citizens, whether it was talking to Martha Gunn in his kitchen or with 'Old Smoaker' his bathing man. One morning he was out for a constitutional – in the perambulatory sense of the word – and, meeting William Tuppen the Quaker builder, somewhat rudely saluted him with, 'How are you, Tuppen?' But the Quaker was well able to speak for himself and answered, 'Very well, thank thee George!'

Although on such good terms with their fellow citizens, the injustice of forcible distraints had not gone away. John Glaisyer Snr, in Third-month 1804, refused to pay the militia rate and, in what was almost an annual ritual, five bushels of flour, valued at 39s 6d, were removed from his shop on the authority of the 'Overseer for Militia Rates' and of the 'Headborough'. The proceedings took place against the background of the Napoleonic Wars, and in the Quaker Yearly Meeting 'Epistle' of 1805, members were reminded not to 'place ... dependence on fleets and armies: be peaceable yourselves in words and actions; and pray to the father of the universe that he would breathe the spirit of reconciliation into the erring hearts of his erring and contending creatures'. Not all Quakers upheld this peaceful testimony and it must have been particularly galling to the righteous when Matthew Bourne Likeman absconded from his apprenticeship and went on board a ship of war. He had denied his fellow-Quakers the possibility of discussing his unhandsome behaviour, and therefore in Seventh-month 1804, 'both for the clearing of truth and our testimony against war', they felt obliged to disown him from membership. Nevertheless, the way was left open for his reinstatement if he should, 'through Divine Assistance, experience a true sense of what he [had] done'.

Brighton Quakers had, since 1792, planned for a new meeting-house. The increasing membership made it necessary, and the old building was in disrepair. A new impetus emerged in 1804 when the Prince of Wales decided he would like to extend his Pavilion Estate. At the Monthly Meeting held at Lewes in Tenth-month 1804, Daniel Hack from the committee appointed to arrange the sale, reported that an agreement had been made with a William Porden, who acted for the Prince. This agreement assigned a field, part of the old North Street property, to the Prince for £800 and, additionally, made available some of the idle portion of the burying ground to give him a gateway to Church Street. While a new meeting-house was being built at Ship Street they met on the same street in a house purchased from John Glaisyer Snr. At a cost of 19s the requisite licence to hold meetings was procured. The land for the new meeting-house had once been owned by Brighton-born William Grover, who was delighted to think of its use for the purpose. The new meeting-house was soon erected and, in 1805, was opened for use.

In 1806, further transactions relating to Friends property took place. Stables had been erected by the Prince's friend Mrs Fitzherbert on New Road. Although there was a passage to the Palace from the stables it is a fallacy that subterranean access existed from the Palace to her house on the Steine. On the other hand, the stables were contiguous to the Quaker Burial Ground, and Quakers found it unacceptable that one of its windows overlooked the ground. Mrs Fitzherbert was anxious to keep her window and the Quaker committee entrusted with the matter, including John Glaisyer Snr and William Tuppen, being 'unwilling to pursue a conduct which may assume the appearance of acting otherwise than neighbourly (notwithstanding injury may arise to the said premises by complying with such request) consents to the window not being stopped up for the present, upon

Map of Brighton showing the site of the old meeting-house (C)

condition of Maria Fitzherbert agreeing to pay one penny per month for such permission'. William Tuppen was requested to take a copy of the committee's minute to Mrs Fitzherbert to see if its suggested provisions would be agreeable to her.

The new meeting-house must have seemed to Brighton's Quakers to be symbolic of all the changes and opportunities in the town. Brighton now had a newspaper – the *Brighton Herald* (first published in 1806) – and an Act of Parliament was passed to arrange its new structure of Town Commissioners, of whom several were Quakers. New powers and institutions were needed to deal with the workhouse, street cleaning and planning. The increasing population and the growing tourist and health industries created new challenges, and the commerce of Brighton eventually eclipsed in importance that of Lewes. The influx of wealthy as well as poorer people also had an impact on the town's morals, giving increased scope for philanthropic initiatives. Brighton was known for its radically minded population, and many Quakers who had been loath to participate in explicit political activity had every reason to be more openly sympathetic to political and egalitarian reform.

Young Quakers from other parts of the country often came to Brighton as apprentices or to set up business in the town, and they formed a very creative and energetic group. With kindly, illuminated hearts they were 'anxious to forward the Kingdom by serving their fellow creatures in the town'. One of them was Isaac Bass, who came from Hitchin Monthly Meeting. As was the custom, he brought with him a certificate of his good behaviour, that he had left no debts and was free of marriage engagements. His certificate was accepted at Monthly Meeting on 20 Second-month 1804, and John Glaisyer Snr and William Tuppen were 'desired to inform him', and also to issue an acknowledgement to Hitchin Monthly Meeting.

A second young Quaker to become noteworthy was Grover Kemp. In 1806, aged fourteen, he arrived in Brighton to start an apprenticeship with John Glaisyer Jnr, a chemist and druggist. He entered into partnership with his employer, and then continued the business. Conscious of the gaps in his own education, he set out on a course of self-improvement, and got up early every morning to study chemistry and to learn some Greek. Kemp also wrote essays, which apparently showed much thoughtfulness. In 1816, he married Susanna Horne of Arundel. He was only nineteen when his voice was heard for the first time in the ministry in his own Meeting and he was eventually, in 1823, 'recorded in the ministry' by the Monthly Meeting, which in Quaker parlance means that his evident gift was noted as 'acceptable'.

In 1811, a balance of one acre of the North Street end of the old meeting-house property was sold for £2,000 and the money was used towards the new Ship Street property, for which two houses were pulled down. The Brighton Meeting showed a healthy rise in numbers, and by 1812 there was something in the region of 109 members. John Glaisyer Snr, whose property had formed the nucleus of the new site died, aged 73, in the following year. He had taken a prominent part in the affairs of the Monthly Meeting and had been a minister for 27 years. 'He was a striking example of circumspection and watchfulness over his words and actions: tender of exposing the failings or weaknesses of others: yet faithful in offering private reproof or counsel, when duty required it.'

Also in 1813, Thomas Shillitoe (1754-1836) visited Brighton. He was a Quaker minister who had travelled widely on the Continent and in Ireland, where he visited as many public houses as he could – not in pursuit of the drink that inebriates but does not cheer, but to give quiet advice to publicans about moderation. His mission in Brighton was somewhat different. With the Quaker penchant for 'speaking truth to power' he decided his duty was to speak to the Prince Regent, about the moral responsibilities of his position. Shillitoe was a man of an almost neurotic sensitivity; the decision was for him nervously fraught, but having tested his insight he was indefatigable. When he arrived in Brighton, he met with the local Quakers who had the required essential local knowledge. At first, they could not see any necessity for his visit and endeavoured to persuade him to think some other way about it, even volunteering to present his message for him.

Thomas Shillitoe was, however, not to be dissuaded, and Brighton Quakers agreed a delegation to accompany him. The plan was to meet and have horses ready when he felt the moment right, and they would wait till the Prince emerged for his early morning ride and speak to him then. But the Prince went on another route altogether, and the Quakers had great ground to cover. George and his party were riding too fast, and the Quakers were somewhat slow. Shillitoe, with a great impulse of energy, galloped forward and passed the Royal party, who were heading over the Downs, but by then he had no breath left to give his message, and had to trot ahead even further to recover himself. The Prince Regent was not pleased, and said he was pressed for time, but he did agree that the written message should be passed to another of the party, Colonel Bloomfield, which is what was done. However Thomas Shillitoe then insisted on speaking to the Colonel to be reassured that George would certainly read the letter. Shillitoe felt afterwards that there had been a practical result to the good moral advice given in it.

In such a small town as Brighton then was, encounters between the contemporary Royals and Friends and other citizens were not unusual; the Quakers adhered with dignity to their democratic but mannerly customs in dealing with them, and this resulted in mutual respect. At the time the fashionable world enjoyed hobby-horse racing round the Level, to the north of the Palace, and frequently went to visit the nearby Morris's Royal Repository – a great toy shop which was often very crowded. William, Duke of Clarence, who later became King William IV, and who had a reputation for dalliances with women, was frequently there and was once struck by the entrance of three Quakeresses. The two older ones were looking at some particular object and 'His Royal Highness' turned to the youngest, aged fourteen. Using Quaker phraseology he said, 'I see that thou art not above the vanities of the gay world.' The fair young Quakeress answered nothing, but the matron under whose care she was gave a severe look more expressive than words. The Duke felt it and, to make up for his remark, bought a handsome workbasket and requested the elderly Friend for permission to present it to the young girl. Laconically, she replied 'She will receive it and thank thee, Friend.' The basket was taken with the same courtesy as had been given and there the matter ended.

Among several other stories reflecting positive contacts between Friends and 'the powers that be' is one from 1814, when Tsar Alexander I of Russia came to England on a fact-finding mission to help him improve the conditions of his people. Initial and important contacts occurred with a number of Quakers including William Allen, the London chemist and philanthropist. William Allen (1770–1843) was a friend and business contact of John Glaisyer Jnr, the Brighton pharmacist, and arranged for the Tsar to visit him on his way home. In the event that visit was not possible, but Brighton's loss was Amberstone's gain. When the Tsar, with his sister the Duchess of Oldenberg, passed through Amberstone, near Hailsham, it happened that Nathaniel and Mary Rickman were standing at their garden gate to see the great man go by. Clad, as they were, in traditional Quaker garb they were easily recognisable, and the Tsar ordered his carriage to stop, asking if he might visit them in their house. No sooner asked than done, and a welcome was extended. The Tsar was entertained to lunch and shown over the plain and neat dwelling. Then the Tsar shook Nathaniel Rickman's hand, and the Duchess of Oldenberg kissed Mary Rickman, and they all waved goodbye as the carriage rattled on to Dover in a cloud of dust.

Grover Kemp, young as he was, did not waste any time getting involved on the philanthropic front. In 1817, aged only 25, Kemp worked with Daniel Pryor Hack and other Quakers and leading Brightonians to establish the Brighton Savings Bank. Recent legislation underpinned such banks, which were guaranteed by Honorary Trustees, of whom Isaac Bass was one. They were known as 'Penny Banks' and enabled poorer people to save small sums of money and to receive interest on their deposits when the big commercial banks wouldn't even look at them. Humbler working people were thus able to improve their condition by developing positive habits of saving something for a rainy day.

Noticeable among his fellow-Quakers for his entrepreneurial spirit was John Hilton (d.1865). His bakery business at 10 West Street was inaugurated in 1815, but in 1821 he opened a business as grocer and tea dealer at the corner of Gardner Street and Church Street. He owned five plots of building land in Gardner Street, and after building his shop sold the others. The site was seen as remote at the time and there were few houses there. All these Quaker families were intermarried. This was partly a result of refusing to recognise that paid clergy should have a role in marriage, which was regarded as being between the parties involved, including the worshipping community and the Divine Power; this did not include a clergyman.

Another Quaker family prominent in the commerce and philanthropy of Brighton over several generations was the Hack family, which originated in Chichester and Hampshire. Daniel Pryor Hack (1794–1886) was the son of the previously mentioned linen draper of East Street, Daniel Hack, and Sarah Pryor, and he was born when the town had only 6,000 inhabitants. Aged only eight years old he was sent to school in Rochester, and was then apprenticed to a Friends drapery business in Chelmsford. In his twentieth year he was drawn for the militia, but he refused to serve and

Daniel Pryor Hack 1794–1886

was imprisoned. In 1815, when his father became sick, he returned to his native town and, with his brother William, helped rescue the family drapery and linen business, which had been imperilled by an unfaithful foreman. In 1817, soon after the death of his dear sister and his mother he joined a Mr Vallance in running an adult evening class, and did not neglect attending the Friends mid-week meeting for worship. He worked hard for the British and Foreign School Society, which had schools in several places including Middle Street and North Road, and he also worked for the Society for the Suppression of Climbing Boys, which saved children from being sent up chimneys to clean them.

Eliza Carter (d.1878), daughter of James Carter of James's Street, Brighton, married Daniel Pryor Hack in 1819 when she was aged 23. Her own mother had died when she was only eight years old, and aged ten, she had been sent to the Mount School, York, where she sometimes sat alone and read her Bible in an apple tree. On her return to Brighton, she helped in her father's shop and took care of a beloved aunt. Her twenty-first year was memorable when she openly professed Christ in meetings for worship and was eventually acknowledged in the ministry. Humble about her place in the Meeting, she took a caring role for her husband's blind father as well as the men and apprentices busy at the business, and employed about the house. Careful of the reputation of others, she was faithful to warn those she saw to be in danger of doing themselves spiritual hurt.

From 1823, the year of his father's death, Daniel Pryor Hack felt called to preach the Gospel and was recorded in the ministry. Later, in 1827, he handed over his profitable business to his brother, William Hack, which left him more free time to devote to ministry and philanthropic work. It also left his wife free to work among the sick and poor. A memorable call on him was when a governess was sentenced to prison. She had been at the school Eliza Hack attended as a child and, during a Quarterly Meeting visit Daniel Pryor Hack visited her at the prison at Horsham. When the time came for her release, she was extremely ill and he read to her from the Bible, 'Comfort ye, Comfort ye, my people, saith your God. Speak ye comfortably to Jerusalem and cry unto her that her warfare is accomplished, that her iniquity is pardoned.' The governess died an hour afterwards; Daniel and Eliza were humbled under a sense of their own liability to err and were very tender towards the erring and slow to impute unworthy motives.

Perhaps around 1823 also, the wife of Chamerouzoff, one of the musicians in George IV's private band, called into the Hacks' drapery shop and asked that Daniel Pryor Hack would visit her husband. He felt no big inclination to oblige but Chamerouzoff had fallen sick and Hack, having a smattering of French, went to read to him from a French Bible. Chamerouzoff, convinced that his Saviour was sufficient for him and therefore that he needed no priest, was consumptive and dying. He asked Daniel Hack to take care of his wife and child. Daniel Pryor Hack did exactly that and had the child educated at Quaker William Allen's Industrial School at Lindfield; when he grew up he became the secretary of the British Anti-Slavery Society.

Daniel Pryor Hack actively helped the educational schemes of William Allen, about whom a few words should be said since he was friendly with many of the Brighton Quakers, and occasionally took part in events organised in the town. William Allen had a genius and energy for philanthropy, and travelled in many countries including Ireland and Russia to advance understanding towards the relief of poverty, the promotion of education and peace, and the reform of prisons. He hoped to improve the conditions of people so that they would not be forever trapped in poverty, and to this end pioneered an industrial school at Lindfield. There, the pupils learned useful skills such as that of printing, and you can often come across the tiny volumes of Quaker texts that they produced.

Another Quaker associated with William Allen in the setting of Brighton was Elizabeth Fry (1780–1845). Almost inevitably her name emerges throughout contemporary Britain, although, in this case, not in connection with prisons. Her first visit to Brighton was because of her own bad health, and her family encouraged her to visit 'Dr Brighton' and recuperate; even then she would not rest, but sought fields for active service. As soon as word got round that she was in town, queues of poor people came to seek help at the door of the house where she was staying. Elizabeth Fry had only recently spoken to the prominent preacher Dr Thomas Chalmers (1780–1847) about ways of helping the poor so they would not suffer any loss of self-respect. Professional beggars often used up funds that would otherwise have gone to the truly needy, who were too proud to seek such aid. The solution she came up with in Brighton was to divide up districts and get ecumenical teams to co-operate in visiting each house to see what practical needs could be met. A savings scheme was also set up; for every set amount saved, an arrangement was made to top it up with a premium, designed to show the practical effects of saving as a form of self-help. Elizabeth could not do all this while she was sick, but she returned in 1825 to see how things were going, when the First Annual Report of the Brighton District Society, as it was known, was issued. Grover Kemp was one of its vice-presidents and so was Henry M. Wagner, the Vicar of Brighton, who had only taken up office the year before. At the first meeting William Allen came along to give his support also. This Society proved a template for others set up in England.

Elizabeth Fry had been in the habit of opening her window whenever she felt faint and discovered that the fresh Brighton sea air helped to revive her. Often she noticed a lone coastguard or 'blockade man' pacing the pebbly beach, and thought to herself that his job must be very isolating, night and day with little human contact except with smugglers. She wondered how a coastguard otherwise passed his time, and when she was out for a drive she stopped her carriage and attempted to speak to one. But he was a man of honour and, being forbidden by the regulations from speaking to strangers, would not give her any information. Fearing she might have got him into trouble, she gave him her card and asked him to tell his commanding officer what had occurred. The commanding officer called on Elizabeth Fry later, and as a result of their pleasant conversation, libraries were set up for coastguards, and a welcome supply of Bibles obtained for them from the Brighton Auxiliary of the British Bible Society.

Isaac Bass, whom we have already mentioned, was another Brighton Quaker who had a special input into the town's life. His grocery business was at Brighton-place, and in 1812 he had married Sarah, the daughter of John and Sarah Glaisyer of Brighton. They were well matched to help each other in the spiritual life and its practical expression. Sarah's parents had helped her to an intimate knowledge of the scriptures and trained her in the value of silent worship. She was active in and initiated some charitable undertakings, and with five or six young men boarding in her house she needed regularity and method, clear judgement and quick perception to enable her to carry out her domestic and philanthropic work. In all this she never neglected going on one side for prayer and self-examination. The kind friend and adviser of the distressed, the widow and the orphan, she was looked on as a mother by many not related to her. Isaac Bass, for his part, was a great supporter of the public charities and was a Governor of the Sussex County Hospital and of the Brighton Dispensary, as well as contributing to many other local institutions.

This was a period when anxiety about the continuing use of slavery in the British Colonies provoked people to organise to persuade Parliament to legislate for its abolition. The London Yearly Meeting of 1824 took the initiative in restarting the campaign and issued regular petitions. Local anti-slavery societies, in co-operation with other citizens, were also established. It was thought in 1826 that Brighton had been slower than other towns in coming forward in the cause. But there were no limits to the numbers of people who would enthusiastically show their disapproval of the slavery system if someone would start the ball rolling. When Mr W. Clarkson, a fellow-worker of the veteran abolitionist Thomas Clarkson (1760–1846), came to the town in 1826, a petition was promptly promoted and left for signature at the Old Ship Tavern. It was signed by almost all the clergy and middle-class inhabitants of the town, and attracted the support of the Jewish community too. Brighton Quakers were active in this new phase of the anti-slavery campaign but local newspapers do not give enough information to determine how significant their intervention was, and give very inadequate reports of the anti-slavery society that is presumed to have existed. John Glaisyer and Isaac Bass were certainly among the activists and their names occur when they forwarded or supported resolutions. Daniel Pryor Hack is remembered as an anti-slavery activist too. Activities were not confined to Brighton, and in 1833 Shoreham was the venue for a meeting called by the local clergyman, where the Friend Samuel Lidbetter supported resolutions, and Isaac Bass was one of the two representatives appointed as delegates to travel to London.

Quaker anti-slavery protest was not merely rhetorical but was also practical and personal, involving abstinence from the use of slave products such as sugar. Phoebe Glaisyer (d.1904), originally from Hitchin, well remembered 'the peculiar flavour given to gooseberry or apple puddings when sweetened with honey, there being no sugar on the table. They were not nearly so nice.' A degree of success was achieved in 1834 when the slaves in the Colonies were reclassified as 'apprentices'. However, there was little real change in their status and a scandalous government reparation to slave-owners, so the battle went on. The date was seen as memorable in Quaker circles and in the Lewes Quaker school the pupils were taught Jane Taylor's verses about 'The Little Negro Boy': 'It was on the first of August eighteen hundred thirty-four / We told the poor black people we would serve them so no more.'

When cholera hit Britain and Ireland in 1831–2, a Board of Health was set up in Brighton, and the town fortunately remained free of the disease. The healthy winds and chalk Downs were said to have prevented its spread, but the sewerage of the town was inadequate to the point of being almost non-existent, with cesspits at the door. Disease could spread rapidly under such conditions. It was in the interest of every class and individual to spend time, money and effort to cleanse the town and be ready to care for the victims – for all were potential victims. Already, concerned citizens had put their efforts into the provision of hospitals and health facilities. Other causes of disease were bad diet and housing. The workhouse system was not the most attractive and had been open to abuse, but some attempted to humanise its operations and properly supervise it. There was always a clear need for hospitals and ancillary medical charities and Brighton Quakers did their utmost to help in the establishment of these, and their names appear frequently in subscription lists.

It was old age and not cholera that caused the death in 1832 of a number of ancient Friends. Quite early in the year, Sarah Glaisyer, the widow of John Glaisyer Snr, died. She had joined Friends in 1769 and had been an Elder for many years. Although she was hardworking and had the care of a big family she never used this as an excuse and was always punctual in attending meetings for worship and the Women's Meetings. With her husband, she tried to bring up their children to respect and be conscious of the Lord as was consistent with their Quaker commitment. She often expressed her earnest desire for the best welfare of her children and grandchildren in an affectionate and impressive manner. Often she felt a humbling sense of weakness and unworthiness, remarking that she had nothing to look to but the mercy of her dear Redeemer. Her friends Richard and Jane Patching died later in the year, within a few days of each other, and were buried together. They had joined Quakers forty years before, and there was a big attendance at their funeral, with many shops closed on the occasion as a sign of respect.

From his first arrival in Brighton in 1804, Isaac Bass had, like his co-religionists, been the victim of continuing distraints of his goods. Regularly every year, candles, hams and cheeses flew out of his grocery shop at the hands of the distrainers, but he was not discouraged from playing a constructive part in the civic affairs of his adopted town; during 1824, and for many years afterwards, he was one of the Town Commissioners. With his fellow-townspeople, and in defence of his own interests, he was a staunch opponent of church rates or, as Quakers said, 'church-rates – so-called'. In 1832, the opposition to church rates became more vociferous, and Isaac Bass and John Hilton were prominent in the resistance campaign. Isaac Bass was credited with obtaining Brighton's eventual relief from church rates. His great advantage was seen as his being always equable in his temper without ever being bland or suave. His manner was simple and his address was laconic. If his exterior was rough, however, the kernel was sweet.

Isaac Bass began to try his hand in more directly political campaigns using the improved democracy offered by an extended suffrage. Following the passing of the Reform Act in 1832 Brighton became a two-seat borough, and Isaac Bass seconded the nomination of George Pechell, whom he supported through several elections. Captain Pechell was eventually elected in

1835, with 961 votes. Isaac Bass was a Liberal, as would have been most Quakers. With a change in atmosphere among Quakers as well as in the country at large, many Friends took a greater part in political matters. Anti-slavery activism was a form of para-politics that must have encouraged them to do this, but some Quakers still had reservations about participating in party politics.

Bass also took a very practical interest in the poor and disadvantaged, and especially during 1836 when, following a period of bad weather the Guardians of the Poor organised distributions of soup. Not only was he the Treasurer of the General Relief Committee set up for this, but he also provided vessels for boiling the soup, and premises in Spring Gardens for the distribution itself. Isaac Bass remained the Committee's treasurer until 1853. Perhaps, the most significant visible impact Isaac Bass's life had on the shape of modern Brighton was in the road he created to make a more suitable approach to the Town Hall – this had been surrounded by tumbledown houses. In 1838, he bought the old Vicarage and its land to form the wide

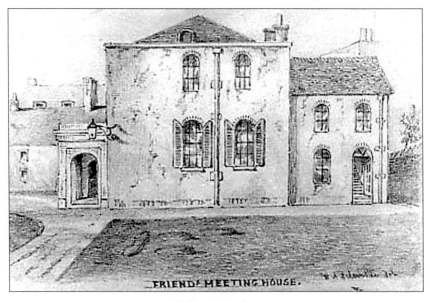

Ship Street meeting-house

approaches from East Street and Ship Street now known as the Bartholomews and Prince Albert Street. Later, he bought what had been the Wigney's Bank in East Street and threw it down to provide an approach to East Street and the Town Hall from the Old Steine. Isaac Bass also provided the houses that were knocked down to link Ship Street and Black Lion Street, thus forming the west end of Prince Albert Street.

Another Friend who was a Town Commissioner was John Patching. With his brother, Richard Patching Jnr, they were chosen in 1836 to superintend the collection of the coal tax. The Town Commissioners had previously let the collection out on sureties. It was very profitable, at the rate of 6d per chaldron of coal or culm landed from vessels discharging from the sea in front of the town. Although the tax was very unpopular and its collection had always met opposition, Richard Patching succeeded so well that the take rose by 10 per cent in the first year he held the office.

In 1838, a more decisive and determined phase of the anti-slavery movement began. A huge petition was got up to send to London. Women organised their own separate one. On Tuesday, 27 February 1838, at two o'clock, a public meeting of 'The Friends of the Negro' was held at the Town Hall to hear Mr J. Scoble share information and personal experience about the Negro 'Apprentices' of the West Indies where he had recently been visiting. The High Constable presided and several Ladies were also present. John Glaisyer Jnr was one of those noted as being present, and Grover Kemp was, in 1840, one of the Brighton Friends who attended the great Anti-Slavery Convention in London.

Grover Kemp often had reason to travel, and when the London–Brighton railway line was being built, welcomed the prospect of being able to travel more easily. Its opening introduced ever more visitors to the town and increased the number of workers who had built and ran the line. On 21 September 1841, the new line opened on a day that started foggy. Grover Kemp had intended to be on the first train, but he suddenly remembered his young family and thought of the danger posed by tunnels. He decided he had no right to take an unnecessary risk and so, on that day at least, travelled in the traditional way by coach. The new railways eventually opened a new sphere for service for Grover Kemp, a recorded minister among Quakers, and he often preached at religious meetings held for the men building the lines to Brighton, Lewes and Hastings. This proved to be the beginning of a long-standing link between Quakers and the railway workers. Grover Kemp also held meetings in barns and storehouses in villages around Brighton, and especially wherever there were neglected meeting-houses. Minutes often record his 'liberation' to hold such meetings for young people or at places such as Rottingdean.

Quakers, not being much given to frivolity, tended to be interested in scientific and educational subjects. Their thoughtful character was reinforced by avoiding dancing, drinking or novels. The Brighton Scientific and Literary Association (BSLA), which met at the Royal Albion Hotel, was set up in 1841 and on its committee of management were Isaac G. Bass (son of the Isaac Bass we have heard about), and John Glaisyer of St James's Street. An outgrowth of this was the Brighton and Hove Natural History and Philosophical Society, a founder of which was Arthur Wallis, a young scholarly Quaker and proprietor of a lithographic printing company in Bartholomews. Another activist of Quaker antecedents was John Horne, and it was said of him that, if Sussex were to be destroyed by a tidal wave, he would be able to reconstruct it. Arthur Wallis usually set up and superintended the botanical collections for the soirees of the BSLA. Botany was his favourite subject and he also helped to found the Horticultural and Floral Society. He died young of a disease of the lungs, leaving his wife Hannah to rear their five children, one of whom, Mary Ann Wallis (1847–1919), became well known as an educationalist, in spite of her blindness.

The practical needs of people were great and the dangers posed by alcoholic drink to health and families were seen as one of the chief enemies of human happiness. Many Quakers, mostly temperate anyway, went the extra step and took a pledge of total abstinence, and used every endeavour to raise the consciousness of Brightonians on the issue. Grover Kemp was one of these Friends, and he wrote an earnest appeal, 'A Tract for the Season', to encourage watchfulness against the usual excesses of Christmas. John Hilton Jnr (1820–1908), son of John Hilton Snr, took the total abstinence pledge in 1840 and in 1844–5 promoted and was secretary of the Brighton Friends Association for Diffusing Information on the Principle of Total Abstinence from Intoxicating Liquors (BFADIPTAIL), and of the Brighton Temperance Society. In First-month 1846 the BFADIPTAIL issued its first report. On its committee were Edward Lucas (Treasurer), Richard Patching Jnr and John Hilton Jnr (Secretaries), and Grover Kemp and Thomas Glaisyer. At a later stage of his teetotal career, and following an illness, John Hilton, as a token of thanks for his services to Brighton, was given a purse of gold and an address at the Town Hall attended by 400 people.

Richard Patching Jnr remained a staunch abstainer all his life. He wanted not just to alleviate poverty but to prevent it, and gave great support to all organisations promoting thrift. He was Secretary of the first and second building societies to be established in Brighton in 1843 and 1845; and in 1850 and for long years afterwards was Chairman of the Brighthelmston Jubilee and Accident Fund, which helped those who might otherwise have been plunged into poverty by some accident or temporary distress.

The chief plan of the BFADPTAIL was to circulate temperance tracts and periodicals, but it also organised six public meetings. Members distributed these tracts in Brighton and its neighbourhood, at the barracks and guard stations, to railway workers and to schools. They gave a quantity to the Wesleyan Tract Society and to the Brighton Society for the Suppression of Intemperance. Among Quakers, several temperance monthly periodicals were distributed. The committee in its report concluded that the evil effect of alcohol affected every class and admitted how limited were their efforts, but 'under divine blessing … felt some little good may hereby be effected'.

In 1846, many Quakers were galvanised to articulate once more their ancient testimony against war. There were rumours of war that would not go away, and in Brighton Militia Clubs were set up to facilitate government legislation for a draft. The Peace Society, supported by many Quakers, initiated protests and over eighty anti-militia meetings were reported nationally. John Jefferson, of the Peace Society, addressed one such meeting at the Brighton Town Hall. It was not very well reported in the Brighton newspapers except in attacks on the peace viewpoints advocated. Peace activists were accused of being naïve and unrealistic, and for failing to distinguish between defensive and offensive warfare. It was cryptically suggested that a time might come when even Quakers might take up arms!

4.
IN QUEEN VICTORIA'S REIGN (1837–1901)
1853–99
'Be of good cheer'

THE physical, spiritual and communal centre of the Brighton Quakers was the meeting-house at Ship Street, where they resorted several times a week for the meeting for worship, and usually also for the regular business meetings to 'transact the affairs of the church'. A sketch of the meeting-house made in 1853, by the artist W.A. Delamotte, shows the stove that was once in the centre of the room, and the shutter that could be pulled down to make a separate room for special meetings. At that time there were only 135 regularly assembling for the First-day morning meeting, and 95 for the afternoon meeting. The membership was only modestly greater than at the beginning of the century. It was at this time that a further change occurred, when the Government required Friends to close their burial ground at Ship Street.

View of the inside of the meeting-house by W.A. Delamotte, showing the coal-burning stove and the dividing shutter, 1853

The burial ground, with little tablets set in the wall, was where the garden now is, and had 160 burials recorded there. In 1854 negotiations with Charles Beard, a descendant of the Quaker Beards of Rottingdean, resulted in the purchase of a new burial ground at Black Rock.

One of the first Friends to be buried in the new ground was Isaac Bass. He died on 4 Second-month 1855, at his house in Prince Albert Street, and all the shops there, and in the Bartholomews, were closed for the funeral. Following the meeting for worship, and in spite of the inclement weather, twenty or thirty carriages brought the mourners to the graveside at Black Rock. In 1856, his son, Isaac Gray Bass, became Mayor of Brighton. An engineer by profession, Isaac G. Bass was the owner of the *Busy Bee* sloop. He had sold out of the grocery business at nos. 14–15 Market Street, in which he was in partnership with Daniel Hack Jnr (the son of Daniel Pryor Hack) and Marriage Wallis, and had moved to Rottingdean. He had shares in a coalmine and in a nail manufactory. When his first wife died he married again, and later, moved with his family to Cumbria, sending all his goods round in the *Busy Bee*.

In 1857, two years after the death of Isaac Bass, Grover Kemp sought a 'minute of unity' from the Lewes Monthly Meeting for a visit to the West Indies. Noted as an anti-slavery worker, he was also a minister among Quakers, and had visited co-religionists in the South of France and in Ireland. But, in this new venture, he hoped to see how the lives of the freed slaves had improved. There were sometimes between seven and eight hundred people at his meetings in the West Indies and he felt united in Christian fellowship with many of the missionaries he met. He was accompanied by William Holmes of Alton and by his son, Caleb Rickman Kemp (1836–1908), who had only recently been acknowledged as a minister.

Although the slaves had finally been released in the British Colonies, slavery was still a universal problem, especially in America. The American Civil War (the first shots of which were fired in 1861) had other causes besides freedom for slaves, but Brighton Quakers, like their co-religionists elsewhere, wished to do as much as they could to help the victims of slavery and the war. Some American Quakers organised an escape route for slaves fleeing the southern states, and in Brighton funds were raised and bundles of clothing sent to help them. At various times in the 1860s, at the request of the Monthly Meeting, assistance was channelled to the 'Negro Emancipation Fund' and to the 'Freedman's Aid'.

Other Quakers continued to promote works of kindness on the home front and in such ways to transmit the Gospel. Robert Horne Penney (d.1902) was one of the most influential Brighton Quakers in the latter half of the nineteenth century. He was born at Poole and apprenticed in the sail-making business, and in 1852 he settled at Southwick. Married to Lucy Rickman Lucas he succeeded to the shipping business of her father Edward Lucas, who headed off to Hitchin and joined the banking firm of Sharples & Co. Like many before him Robert Horne Penney found Brighton a very congenial place to live and he was always interested in outdoor activities – in the sea, the river and country life; as owner and manager of a large shipping fleet he was a member of the Shoreham Harbour Trustees. Of the eight children born to himself and his wife, five died young.

Each week Robert Horne Penney, with his family, drove the four miles by the coast road from Southwick to Brighton for the meeting for worship, leaving his wagonette in the stable yard of the Clarence Hotel; sometimes he walked there by himself for the evening meeting also. In politics he was a Liberal, and was a dedicated teetotaller since he signed the Pledge in 1841. Prepared for every emergency, he always had on hand a selection of pamphlets on peace, smoking and temperance. His little son Robin would have a weekly confidence for Martin Robinson of Saddlescombe. Once it was, 'Martin Robinson, our cat ran up the chimney, but papa got the tongs and tonged her down!'

Maude Robinson (d.1950), the daughter of Martin Robinson, had vivid memories of him driving the family in a carriage from Saddlescombe to Brighton for 'First-day' meeting for worship. They would come into town down the Dyke Road, and past St Nicholas's church to North Street, where they once met a team of six red oxen drawing a wagon of dirty ice. She was only four years old when she first attended meeting at Ship Street, and it was regarded as a privilege – the children remaining for the whole time in the sometimes totally silent meetings. She enjoyed the warm and kindly greeting from the Ship Street Friends. One old farmer's wife from the eastern Downs used to slip a little parcel of barley sugar into her hand each week for years. The Robinsons also travelled to Brighton each Fifth-day for the morning meeting for worship. After that they would do their important shopping. The Brighton drapers' shops were small, and the owner would bustle forward to serve the quiet lady in the Quaker bonnet who had such a large family, and knew just what she wanted.

Two very senior figures in the Brighton Meeting were Daniel Pryor Hack and his wife Eliza, who lived at 'Fircroft', Withdean. A visitor to the house described her impressions:

I shall never forget my first visit to this home and my first sight of real Friends. The grandfather and grandmother were in the drawing room overlooking their pretty garden and the sight of their calm, sweet faces, enhanced by the mother's picturesque costume of grey, with snowy kerchief pinned over her breast; and the 'How dost thou do, Agnes Johnston?' finished my conquest, and I have loved Friends from that moment.

Eliza Hack practised early rising and economy of time, reading the Scriptures in private retirement. She was often Clerk or Assistant Clerk at the London Yearly Meeting. When it was beginning to become more acceptable for men and women to sit together in meeting, instead of on opposite sides of the room, many Brighton Quakers looked forward to the occasion, but hesitated to offend Eliza Hack. She, understanding their reluctance, said that she and her husband always preferred to sit together, and thus left the way open for others to do likewise.

Their son, Daniel Hack Jnr, went to extremes in his early temperance enthusiasm, and when for some reason his father bought property in Black Lion Street, including a Public House, he joined a number of young people in carrying the barrels out and pouring the contents down the drains, much to the horror of some of the townspeople. Later, when much older he admitted that the proceeding may have been unwise. Some Quakers were resistant to temperance reform, and had plausible arguments in favour of alcohol. Maude Robinson tells of one Quaker of that mind who suddenly appeared wearing the Blue Ribbon of a teetotaller, and her father Martin Robinson asking 'What, have thee come to that, Richard?', and sharing the sadness of the reply: 'Oh, if I had only seen it when thee did, Martin.' His son had died of alcoholic poisoning in a colonial street, whereas Martin's four sons were all staunch abstainers, and were safe at home.

Brighton was well known for the exceptional number of its private fee-paying schools and a number of Quakers ran some of these. Maude Robinson remembered the boys' school run by Frederick Taylor and the girls' school run by Emily Sanders. The pupils were allotted a particular place in the Meeting. The school run by Bedford Gilkes was attended by Caleb Rickman Kemp, who was so impressed by his teacher that he later called his house in Lewes 'Bedford Lodge'. A tragedy occurred in Frederick Taylor's school in 1866, when four of his pupils, including brothers John Dann, aged fourteen, and Samuel Tully Dann, aged eleven, of Nutfield, Surrey, were drowned in an accident. Frederick Taylor closed his school after this, but continued as a minister among Quakers.

The education of women was a central task among Quakers. Maude Robinson was sent to boarding school at Lewes, Eighth-month 1872. The school was run on very traditional Quaker lines by Rachel Special and Mary and Catherine Trusted, who were utterly conscientious and kindly teachers. They dressed in the plainest, neatest gowns and wore muslin or net caps, addressing their pupils in the correct way as 'Thou' and 'Thee'. Maude once broke a favourite vase and feared blame, but Catherine Trusted laughed and said 'That's the way to treat small misfortunes.' Instead of dancing, which was regarded with disapproval, the children learned deportment, and heard mildly scientific lectures on light, heat and electricity. Maude did not like the French master, who seemed to have favourites among the girls. Apart from French, the pupils learned, among other subjects, handwriting, needlework, German, Geography and English Grammar. An important event, perhaps, Maude Robinson supposed, the most important in her life was when she heard a visiting Quaker minister in meeting. It was not so much his words as where they came from that reached her. She felt she could lay her sins at the foot of the Cross; from then on she quietly dedicated herself to Jesus Christ, who, through thick and thin, whether successfully or otherwise, she followed throughout the rest of her life.

Among the younger Friends in 1870, was Daniel Hack Jnr. He had been educated at Isaac Brown's of Hitchin and by Bedford Gilkes at Brighton; following an apprenticeship to William Sparkes of Worcester, he returned to his home town and became a partner with his relative Marriage Wallis in the grocery business originally set up by Isaac Bass. Married to Martha Gibbins of Birmingham in 1861, they both shared an interest in the German language and enjoyed a great unity of purpose and comradeship. This knowledge of German came in very handy in 1870, when the Franco-Prussian war was raging. This was to him, as to other Quakers, a call not to arms, but to put peace into action. On 19 Eleventh-month 1870, under the auspices of the Friends War Victims Fund, he went to Metz to administer relief to the suffering non-combatants, and wrote a series of letters about the work to the *Sussex Daily News*. All Brighton waited anxiously for news, and more so when he fell sick; in Twelfth-month his wife and sister went out to nurse him.

In the 1870s, the Brighton Young Friends organised many activities of their own. Mary Hack, Daniel Hack's sister, used to join them, never feeling age to be an inhibiting factor in the way of free expression. The impact of the wider Evangelical movement focused belief and renewal. The search for learning by these Quakers was not confined to themselves, and they tried to share its benefits with others, seeing it as the key to social reform. Education would enable the under-privileged to help themselves.

A natural instrument for educational concern in the 1870s was in Adult Schools, and Brighton Quakers used their Ship Street premises for these. They provided a basic education with opportunities to discuss social issues and to study the Bible. Adult education, and what was politely called 'extension work', was somehow unintentionally conflated. For traditional Quakers, the encounter with people who did not necessarily share their own assumptions of class or wealth, proved stimulating. The great bulk of the Meeting's membership at this time was made up of traditional 'birth-right' Friends, and there had been little intake from outside, but the Adult School incidentally brought in an influx of new members. Marriage Wallis, recorded as a minister in 1870, was very concerned to guide them and enjoyed explaining the Scriptures, which focused the power in his ministry.

The increase in the numbers attending the Adult School at Ship Street led to a decision to build an extension to the meeting-house. On 16 Fourth-month 1876, Brighton Preparative Meeting appointed a committee of Robert Horne Penney, Alfred Lucas, Marriage Wallis, Richard Patching and Charles Edward Clayton to consider 'the desirability of increasing the accommodation of the premises'. As a result, permission was received from the Monthly Meeting to proceed, and the school block to the north of the meeting-house was built by Holford & Clayton at a cost of £2,420. The premises were in great use, and apart from meetings for 'worship and discipline', adult Bible classes, children's classes, Gospel Temperance Meetings, Women's Mutual Improvement Society meetings and others were held in them. There was also a library at the meeting-house, which Daniel Hack had set up. It was a 'proprietary library' to which every proprietor had a latchkey. It had little in the way of fiction but much in the way of instruction.

Robert Horne Penney and Lucy Rickman Penney moved from Southwick to Brighton in 1871, and in 1876 they built 'Highcroft' in Dyke Road, and lived there. There seemed no limit to the entertaining they did in their gardens. All was seen as part of their work for the Kingdom of Heaven that they sought so diligently to extend on this earth for their Lord. Adult School workers, policemen and their wives, Bible classes, mothers' meetings, the crippled and afflicted, the young and the old were all equally welcomed by Robert Horne Penney. He was a Justice of the Peace and was generous to the poor, also supporting a small host of organisations aimed at the improvement of the social and spiritual life of those he came in contact with.

Visitors from other parts also made a great contribution to Brighton Meeting. One of these was Mary Bowles Browne (1794–1880) from Norwich. A recorded minister, she was accustomed to travelling frequently from place to place. Her lodging at Brighton would become a centre for many, being homely and neat with a plant in the window. She had never many things about her apart from the book she might be reading, and her writing materials. A life-long correspondent, she valued any visits. Since she suffered from deafness there was invariably on her table her 'tube' at hand for callers. Knitting occupied much of her time, and she made kettle holders in two colours as presents for her friends. She also gave little knitted shoes to mothers in the meeting for their babies. Except for her Bible, which she frequently perused, she did not like to burden herself with books but borrowed them from friends, and would rapidly decide whether she liked them or not. After her eightieth year she read all sixteen volumes of the *Penny Cyclopaedia*, and continued to read books in French.

Few people were better loved or esteemed than Richard Patching (1805–85) of Spithurst, near Barcombe, who had been a useful public representative and businessman of Brighton until his death. The family building firm was founded in 1775, at Portland Street, off North Street. A quiet man, his words were always weighty and carefully considered. He was one of the Guardians, who took an interest in the proper running of the workhouse and in the welfare of the poor. During 1873–9 he was Chairman of the Board of Guardians, receiving, in 1879, 4,000 of the ratepayers' votes. A staunch abstainer, Richard Patching had, as a Justice of the Peace, ample experience of the misery and damage that alcohol causes to families and individuals and had read a paper to a Conference of the Poor Law Authorities on the use of alcoholic stimulants in workhouses. He based his paper on a history of the Brighton Workhouse and showed that the removal of alcohol there had been most beneficial. It was the custom in Meeting that when a Friend got down on his knees to pray, the men would rise and remove their hats as a token of respect for the inspiration implied. Maude Robinson, rather irreverently, remembered that sometimes, when Richard Patching took off his hat, he forgot his wig and removed that too!

Another valued Quaker and active citizen of Brighton was Marriage Wallis (1820–97) For 63 years he was closely associated with his relative Isaac Bass, and a number of other Quakers, in schemes to raise up his fellow citizens. His interest in temperance was not confined to the drunkard in the street, but was also towards the help of those secretly in thrall to drink. He was active on the School Board and in the YMCA, of which he was vice-chairman and chairman for thirteen years, in association with his friend and business partner, Daniel Hack. Daniel Hack and Marriage Wallis were among those who, in 1884, donated sums of £500 so that the YMCA could move from its humble premises at Prince Albert Street to Steine House

Through Marriage Wallis's work as a magistrate he tried to help the police and, with Daniel Hack, gave them premises for an institute in Southover Street. Neither did he neglect his own workers. In his little private office and at his own home, young men confessed difficulties and old men spoke of broken-down fortunes and sought advice. However, he was no 'soft-touch' and was quick to detect any hypocrisy. Many remembered his firm handshake with the parting message 'Be of good cheer!' He was a man who valued decisiveness. In a position that required keen business energy, he took upon himself the concerns of his business almost to the point of severe physical illness.

The expansion of the Adult School and demand for its services led to the acquisition of new premises. From 1891, shop premises were rented at 41 Trafalgar Street, and were purchased for £1,150 in 1893 for adult classes and mission meetings. Mission meetings had been run for several years, and were also held at a meeting-house at Black Rock, which had been built in 1859 and enlarged in 1881. These meetings bore little resemblance to traditional Quaker meetings and included hymns and readings with, very often, little silence. They were designed to help in the forwarding of the Gospel, not as proselytising exercises, which Quakers eschewed. However, there was a steady rise in the membership of the Brighton Meeting, which, by 1891, numbered 192 members.

Perhaps one of the most significant Quakers of nineteenth-century Brighton, if we are in any position to evaluate significance on our own limited human scale, was Daniel Hack (d.1910) whose name has recurred in this account. With his wife Martha he took over his father's old house at 'Fircroft'. The Hack family, which has now entirely died out, was responsible for a massive but quiet contribution to Brighton's education, and to all works of quiet charity. During his apprenticeship Daniel Hack had acquired a love of art and found time to study languages, literature and science, and wanted others, less advantaged, to have the same opportunities. He was directly responsible for the provision of museum and library facilities that are with us to this day.

Educational concern was central to Daniel Hack's life, and he founded a Ragged School – a sort of 'dame school'. It was only discontinued in 1871,

Daniel Hack 1834–1910

when it was taken over by the Brighton School Board, of which he was one of the first elected members. Daniel Hack fitted out thirty of Brighton's schools with museums and gave them prints of educational value. The new developing work at York Place School especially appealed to him, since the government had not yet thought much about technical education. Daniel Hack equipped it as a technical school, and paid for every scholar sent to it until the School Board underwrote the work. He founded Hack Scholarships, and science and art scholarships for elementary schools and promoted school libraries. The scholarships were valued at £300 per annum. Not having children of his own, Daniel Hack said he had adopted all the children in Brighton.

Nor was this all. Daniel Hack was closely associated with the Brighton School of Art, and gave £1,000 to the Victoria Lending Library, which formed the basis for the Brighton Public Library. His father, Daniel Pryor Hack, had given £600-worth of books to the original Brighton Free Library, so he was following a well-trodden family path of bibliographic generosity.

During 1881–5 Daniel Hack was a member of Brighton's town council and, later, a Justice of the Peace for the County of Sussex. A strong Liberal, he was notably impartial when presiding over large political gatherings. Not much given to public speaking however, great attention was given to him in meeting for worship when he knelt down in vocal prayer. His crowning act of public generosity was, with his sisters, the giving of nos. 98–99 Trafalgar Street – where the Hack family had once lived – and the enclosure of Pelham Square, to be used by the York Place Secondary School. The Corporation travelled out with the Mayor to Withdean to present him with an address as

an acknowledgement of his exceptional service to Brighton education.

As long as Daniel Hack's sisters,
Priscilla and Mary Pryor Hack, had
lived at 99 Trafalgar Street, it was said
that the brass plate upon its door was
always bright, as if to give a cheerful
welcome, although the name was more
than half-obliterated. The sisters were
quite unaware of it, but to all who
knew them this brass plate, with its
perpetual brightness reflecting the light
of heaven, was emblematic of their
self-effacement. Priscilla and Mary
Pryor Hack were no less remarkable
than their brother in the energy they

Priscilla Hack 1824–1915

used to advance the education and the real happiness of people.

Mary Hack was a moderately prolific author who wrote *Mary Pryor, A
Life Story of a Hundred Years Ago*, a biography of her grandmother pub-
lished in 1887 in London. She also wrote, *Christian Womanhood, Self-
Surrender, Consecrated Women* and *Faithful Service – Sketches of Christian
Women*, which went into print runs of several thousand. One book *Hold the
Fort* warned against the use of stimulants in illness, suggesting helpful sub-
stitutes instead. Active in the Friends Foreign Mission Association, Mary
Hack was also a member of the Local Tract Association and began the
Friends Foreign and Colonial Book Fund, which over the years collected and
sent large quantities of Quaker books to Canada, Australia and other places
where they were unavailable. Acknowledged as a minister in 1888, her ministry was remembered as chiefly intercessory. Prayer became the habit of her
life and was the means of blessing to many. Her prayer in the sick room, by
the empty cradle or chair, was nothing but the simple, genuine opening of a
heart that overflowed.

Priscilla Hack, Mary's sister, was an Elder for 41 years and one of the
readers or assistant clerks at the Women's Yearly Meeting. Active in temper-

ance, education and peace work, as well as work for the Bible Society, she started an evening school for girls and Bible classes on the Sabbath as well as a Mutual Improvement Society for the older members of the Bible class. In these there would be talks on temperance, foreign missions, travel and enlightening subjects. She founded a local widows' society to give practical help to poor women in the first days of their widowhood, and was a member of the Band of Hope, a grouping of teetotal activists. As far back as 1836, she had signed the pledge of total abstinence. Priscilla Hack was educated at Lewes in the school run by Godlee and Dymond, and the pupils remembered the place as 'a happy family of some twenty-four trusted and trusting girls'; Mary Hack, meanwhile, continued her studies at home in Brighton under the guidance of the Hacks' cousin, Charles Tylor, later editor of *The Friend*. The relationship between the two sisters was so strong that Mary Hack described Priscilla as her 'mother-sister'.

An unidentified Quaker reminisced of the sisters:

They had always been unimaginably old – old even for grown-up people – but unlike most grown ups they still retained an intelligent interest in really important things like paper trains that ran across the table on cottons, and painted flower beds. You might snip up as much [paper] as you liked, and use gum freely on the parlour table. I believe that my earliest exploit of a really bold and adventurous character, was to circumnavigate the lily tank parapet with one holding a bunch of me at the back.

Priscilla Hack had brought the young Quaker along the beach on the electric railway, and lifted him up to see the fish in the Aquarium. It was probably Priscilla also who, in 1894, brought him down among the red-sailed fishing boats to see the wreck of the Chain Pier after the Great Storm of that year.

An emergent author among Brighton Quakers was Edward Verrall Lucas (1868– 1938), who lived with his brothers and sisters at St John's Road, west of Adelaide Crescent. His father, Alfred Lucas, was an insurance agent and his mother, Jane (née Drewett) was of the stock of the Rickmans, bankers of Lewes. A thrice-great uncle was Thomas 'Clio' Rickman

(1760–1834) of Lewes, who wore a hat like a beehive, invented a trumpet to increase the sound of a signal-gun, and wrote terrible verse, as well as being a dedicated republican and friend of the renegade Quaker Thomas Paine. Edward Verrall Lucas was born in Kent, but spent all his youthful years in Brighton, and was very proud of his upbringing, regarding himself as a Sussex patriot. A chequered education at eleven different schools might not have boded well but, aged sixteen, he was apprenticed to Treacher's bookshop in 1884. This gave him a chance to nourish his literary bent and, in particular, a taste for the quaint, bizarre

Thomas Hilton 1833-1912

and obscure, often found in Brighton. Two years later he found a position as a journalist with the *Sussex Daily News* and he was soon writing books. He settled in London where, in 1897, he married the daughter of an American colonel. He was a consummate and highly productive writer, whose best-remembered book is, perhaps, *Highways and Byways in Sussex.*

Many Quakers were deeply interested in the world of nature and frequently had minds well stocked with useful facts, and the fruits of thoughtful lives. (Both Martha and Daniel Hack enjoyed gardening, and often went on continental holidays when Martha Hack, who was a skilled painter of flowers, brought back delightful sketches.) Thomas Hilton, (d.1912) attained a local prominence on account of his botanical studies. Born in Church Street he spent most of his life in Brighton, except for a short period attending school in Croydon. Quite late in his life he began the study of botany and when he retired in 1890 he joined the Brighton Natural History Society, finding a role in organising field excursions and becoming its Honorary Curator. In 1894, he started the annual Exhibitions of wild flowers, which were held in the Brighton Museum. Maude Robinson, who shared his interests, occasionally gave him a hand, and he would spend the whole summer gathering specimens, assembling them, and then answering questions about the local flora. He was as modest as his own flowers, and once walked thirty miles to collect a specimen for someone else. When he started his own collection he thought it would be remarkable if he could collect fifty different varieties of wild flower. By the time of his death he had assembled 2,000 varieties, and had even discovered some new species. His herbarium was presented to the South Kensington Museum.

5.
WHY DO THE NATIONS RAGE?
1900–1945
'An underlying sense of goodness'

QUAKERS tried more and more to reach out with material and spiritual help to victims of war and other catastrophes. The Missionary Movement also attracted their attention, and the Missionary Helpers Union and the Friends Foreign Mission Association focused on the mission field and its practical needs. Sometimes evangelistic meetings were held at the Ship Street and Black Rock meeting-houses. The traditional individual philanthropy practised by Friends tended now to find corporate expression through the Meeting itself. Unusually, the Preparative Meeting at Brighton would take on roles not previously imagined for it by Monthly Meeting.

In an age of jingoism, the stand of Quakers against the Boer War did not make them popular. In Brighton, Robert Horne Penney was so much opposed to it (and to all other wars) that he refused to participate in the Queen's Jubilee, because of its association with military display. In the Trafalgar Street Adult School, compulsory military service became the subject of discussion. Other prominent Quakers in Sussex expressed their principled view on the Boer War too. Caleb Rickman Kemp, originally of Brighton, was the Mayor of Lewes in 1900. He carefully asserted his own peaceful variety of patriotism without unduly antagonising his fellow-citizens, and managed to retain their respect.

Memories of the relatively recent Franco-Prussian War and the Boer conflict contributed to the weary sense of more impending international conflict. In Fifth-month 1914, the Preparative Meeting held a special meeting to express Friends' concern to the government and urge support for a neutral position. Sharing the stress that war and peace were in the balance it sent resolutions to the Prime Minister and to the Secretary of State for Foreign Affairs. By Eighth-month, the Meeting was 'under the great shadow of the European War' and a message from the 'Meeting for Sufferings' was read in meetings for worship addressed 'to all men and women of goodwill'.

Some Quakers, however, openly questioned the stance of the Religious Society of Friends on war. For those who valued tolerance, it was a serious question as to how this could be extended to those who disagreed with the traditional testimony of Friends that participation in all war was contrary to the mind of Christ. Several members resigned in Brighton over the issue. Percival Lucas was killed in action, and his brother Edward Verrall Lucas resigned his membership in 1915, on the ground of not wishing to be an 'honorary Friend'; however he exerted himself in relief work in France. The London Yearly meeting of 1915 proved a testing time, and Priscilla Hack, who had been out to Metz during the Franco-Prussian War in 1871, was very anxious that, however its deliberations might proceed, those who could not carry the meeting with them should not become embittered, but might recognise the power that prevailed there.

Brighton Quakers, anxious to do their bit and alleviate the effects of the dreadful warfare, set up a soldiers' Recreation Room at the Friends Institute, an extension of the Ship Street meeting-house. In a report on its work, it was stated that it 'had been a happy home for a large number of soldiers'. Men from about fifty or sixty different regiments used it and many soldiers later wrote in appreciation of the facilities provided. Whilst Brighton Quakers supported all practical relief efforts through the war, there was some resistance to the propagandist aspects of the peace campaign espoused by some. Peace questions were sometimes delegated to the 'Mission Committee' to organise study groups.

A Conscription Act was passed in 1916, which raised great anxieties for Quakers. It gave some recognition of a right to conscientious objection, but some Quakers (and others) took a more extreme view of its provisions and were not willing to undertake any alternative service that released more men to fight. Letters offering advice were distributed to the young men who were members and attenders of Brighton Meeting. When the Government passed its legislation, Brighton Quakers distributed printed advice and inserted notices in the newspapers offering to help Conscientious Objectors (COs). Edward Glaisyer, Brighton-born, was asked by Lewes Quakers to live there and give practical assistance, and he visited the camp at Denton where COs were held.

Military service caused great regret to the Monthly Meeting Overseers when several younger members joined the army. Neville Hampton Wallis was one of those who did so; he was killed in France, aged 26. By 1916–17, some Brighton Quakers had joined the Friends Ambulance Unit and others continued in their useful occupations at home. No members in Brighton suffered arrest or were handed over to the military because of their refusal to fight. Even for Quakers who conscientiously chose to fight in this terrible war, their upbringing was a living influence; 'Little John', in a fragment of autobiography written apparently by a Quaker who joined the army, remembered the influences he received in his childhood from Priscilla and Mary Hack remaining 'like an underlying sense of goodness, at the back of things. It was well to have this abiding knowledge for twenty years, for since then I have seen hell let loose at Suvla Bay.'

A little sign of hope was the birth of Dennis Norman Charlish, who was born in the meeting-house cottage in 1918. His sister was Cherry Charlish (now Wood) and their mother and grandmother were caretaking the meeting-house while their father was away in France. Cherry Wood still has the wedding certificate of her grandparents, who were married 29 Twelfthmonth 1881 in Brighton meeting-house.

No sooner was the war over than Quakers threw their efforts into moves to help the displaced populations of Europe. In 1919, Francis Burrell, in the Brighton Art Gallery, addressed a meeting on the work of the War Victims Relief Committee in France. The Mayor was in attendance and the people gathered subscribed £119 towards relief. The new Mayor of Brighton in 1920 was the Quaker Bernard N. Southall JP, and in an unusual display, the meeting-house was chosen for his inauguration. The meeting for worship proved a very ecumenical occasion, meriting a long, detailed and perceptive description in the *Sussex Daily News*. Outside the meeting-house, a large deputation of unemployed men assembled, and they were received afterwards in the Lecture Room by the Mayor, who promised to do all he could for them.

The spiritual power of the meeting and their faith carried Friends forward as they came to terms with post-war realities. They sought to deepen their individual and corporate spiritual life and express their belief in

Joseph Edward Charlish of Brighton in the County of Sussex, son of William Charlish of Harlestone in the County of Norfolk, and Susan, his wife, and Alice Eliza Herriott of Withdeane in the County of Sussex, daughter of Edward Herriott of Lewes in the County of Sussex, and Eliza his wife (both having duly made known their intention of taking each other in Marriage, and public notice of their said intention having been given, and the needful consent of surviving parents having been signified, the Proceedings of the said Joseph Edward Charlish and Alice Eliza Herriott were allowed by the Monthly Meeting of the religious Society of Friends, held at Brighton in the County of Sussex Now these are to certify that for the solemnization of their said Marriage this Twenty-ninth day of the Twelfth Month, in the Year One thousand eight hundred and eighty-one they the said Joseph Edward Charlish and Alice Eliza Herriott appeared at a public Meeting for Worship, of the aforesaid Society in their Meeting House, in Ship Street Brighton And the said Joseph Edward Charlish taking the said Alice Eliza Herriott by the hand, declared as followeth; — Friends: I take this my friend Alice Eliza Herriott to be my Wife, promising, through Divine assistance; to be unto her a loving and faithful Husband, until it shall please the Lord by death to separate us. And the said Alice Eliza Herriott did then and there, in the said Assembly, declare as followeth; — Friends, I take this my friend Joseph Edward Charlish to be my Husband, promising, through Divine assistance, to be unto him a loving and faithful Wife, until it shall please the Lord by death to separate us. And the said Joseph Edward Charlish and Alice Eliza Herriott as a further confirmation thereof, and in testimony thereunto, did then and there, to these Presents set their hands.

Joseph Edward Charlish

We having been present at the above said Marriage, have also subscribed our Names as Witnesses thereunto, the Day and Year above written.

Alice Eliza Herriott

Elizth Eliza Marriage Wallis	Jno Brown	Thomas Robinson
Jos Tylor	Harriet E. Wallis	Eliza F. Brown	Zephybah Robinson
Anne Whitehead	Lucy R. Penney	Octavius A. Fox	Thomas Wise
Kate Wallis	D. Margaret Penney	Thomas Glaisyer	Mary W.
Mary Hack	Emma Mary Lucas	Priscilla Hack	Sarah Anne Pope
	Mina R. Lucas	John Knowe Glaisyer	Eliza Lewis
	Martin Robinson	Elizth Glaisyer	William Henry Wise
			Mary Wise Junr

Wedding certificate of Joseph Charlish and Alice Herriott, 1881,
witnessed by the members of the Meeting, including Martin Robinson, Priscilla Hack and Marriage Wallis

service to the world around them. Arthur Marsh, a 'birth-right' Friend who spent the first thirty years of his life in Brighton, feels he started attending the Meeting before he was born! His father's name, 'William Marsh', is now resplendent on one of the City of Brighton buses as one of the town's notable citizens. With the other young children, Arthur Marsh used to sit for the first ten minutes of the First-day meeting for worship on the two wooden benches at the back of the meeting-room, where they played and giggled for a bit, before proceeding to the small meeting-room. The older children went upstairs to paint Bible stories or to attend to some junior theology. 'I clearly remember', he writes, 'a regular small episode in the Meeting. A dear elderly Friend who sat just in front of the Minister's Gallery [sometimes called the Elder's Gallery or bench] had a slight nervous cough. He would utter a slight single cough and with a loud click would open a tin of cough sweets. This was followed by the rustling of some crinkly paper and the taking of a sweet. The rustling of the paper and the click of the tin followed again. This only happened once per meeting but you could almost put your watch right by it.' Another dear Friend, somewhat deaf, used to come, as advised, 'with heart and mind prepared', but misconstrued this to bring with him a typed sermon, which was not in keeping with the meeting, and caused one of those unusual events of 'eldering' – which meant requesting him to cease and sit down.

During the period leading up to World War II there was a Young Friends group in Brighton with about twenty members, and they kept a record of their activities. There was also a Peace Committee to further Quaker peace concerns. For a while there was an anxiety to maintain a witness that would not be tarred with a 'left wing' and political brush, but co-operation with the Peace Pledge Union and the Fellowship of Reconciliation proved acceptable. Nevertheless, as we all now know, in spite of their best efforts a terrible war commenced.

This time, compulsory military service was enforced from the very start of the war, and COs again had to appear before tribunals to make their cases for exemption. William (Bill) Barber (d.1986), born at Thakeham, was one such objector. With his wife, Gladys Barber, he had been active in the Peace Pledge Union. The couple had started attending Brighton Meeting in 1938 but William delayed joining until after the war – scorning to use Quaker membership as an umbrella against the call-up. His sturdy independence, however, must have convinced the tribunal of his sincerity and he was permitted to continue the business of 'lighting consultants' and lampshade makers, which he and Gladys Barber had started when scarcely grown up.

Gladys Barber's life of service had started early also, lighting cigarettes for soldiers of the previous world war recovering in what is now Brighton General Hospital. Her first job on leaving school was in the hat department of Ashdown & White and it was there, through the influence of a fellow shop assistant that she became convinced of the wrongfulness of war, and struggle against it became a life passion. Another peace activist described her as the most militant pacifist he had ever come across!

Under these new conditions also, but never daunted by age, remembering the service and sacrifices made by Quaker COs in the previous war, Maude Robinson wrote an article, 'Lest we Forget', which was published in 1940 and detailed something of the struggle in the Yearly Meeting to express a natural love of homeland without compromising loyalty to the Christian gospel of peace. Characteristically, she was prompted to this as she walked on the Downs near her childhood home: contemplating the 'Purple Bugloss' she looked towards Denton, and thought of Edward Glaisyer, and the men once incarcerated there.

During the war Brighton Quakers used the meeting-house premises to help meet the educational and recreational needs of Canadian soldiers stationed in the town. Mabel Notcutt had been involved in the peace movement before the war and joined Brighton Quakers when she was aged 21. She commuted each day to London and when, in 1941, Friends ran their social evenings for soldiers she would come home each Friday and go directly to the meeting-house to play the piano for their dances.

During 1941 Arnold and Dorothy Price were the wardens at the meeting-house, and lived with their daughter Lorna in the cottage. Across the road in Ship Street, over her parents' art shop, lived the young Quaker Pam Manasseh (née Boast). She attended the Middle Street School and then the High School. The two little girls used to play in the meeting-house and garden, where Arnold Price kept pigeons. The two air-raid shelters in the grounds were gloomy and intimidating but possibly marginally less so than the meeting-house! There was no access to the beach and the coast was safe-guarded by huge rolls of barbed wire. Brighton was classified as an 'invasion area' at that time, and eventually the children were evacuated.

6.
A COLLAGE OF MEMORIES
Starting The Next Two Hundred Years
1945–

'Give me a light that I may tread safely'

WITH the cessation of war in 1945 it seemed that a brave new world had emerged, full of possibilities to promote peace and human welfare. The experience of war produced new generations of Quakers resolved to create the conditions where wars could not arise again. One Frank Sainty, travelling on a train, met a young Brighton woman who regretted the lack of educational opportunities in the town. Her plea encouraged him to try and set up a 'People's University', and he went to Friends to suggest part of the meeting-house premises might be the very place for such a venture. Not all Friends agreed, but in 1944 the Friends Centre was set up, with Donald Lawrence, who had represented Quakers in Delhi, as its first Chairman, and Geoffrey and Margery Sedgwick as its first wardens. The aim was to promote the education and development of the whole person, in body, mind and spirit. In the struggle for a better world the non-violent weapons of intelligence could be used through the provision of a wider and deeper education. Among others who were to play a part in running the Friends Centre were Editha Jackson, once a teacher at the Mount School York, and [Mr] Devereux, who was treasurer and legal adviser; Bill and Gladys Barber might be mentioned as central to its work too.

The Friends Centre itself opened in 1945. It was run on a shoestring – funding being a constant concern – but it succeeded in establishing a special place in Brighton life. At first there was a strong family use of the Centre, and a weekly family night for table-tennis and country dancing. The corridors would be piled with clothes for refugees, with collection boxes, and with precious chocolate for starving European children. There were plenty of overseas students in Brighton also, and the Friends Centre had a puppet theatre and held an oceanology weekend with hired boats to study the shore and coastline. There was a painting group and natural history and music groups as well as public lectures and, later, in association with Oxford University, three-year tutorial courses. Language classes, including Esperanto, became more important as time went on and further helped foster international understanding.

Not only was Bill Barber a central figure in the Friends Centre, but he also used his business skills as the convenor of the Finance and Property committee and in numerous other ways. His practicality, business acumen and prudent management of the Meeting's finances were of immense service to Friends. For any committee or business meeting he would do his homework carefully, and then quietly sit back. At the right moment he would slowly rise to offer guidance, as he would say; the over-hasty or inexperienced would be gently pointed in the right direction, the tangled discussion unravelled, the problem calmly and efficiently solved. The list of jobs he did seems endless: Overseer, Elder, governor of the Retreat, initiator of the George Gorman Memorial Fund, funeral arrangements, Home Service, and he positively enjoyed the countless telephone calls involved in such tricky tasks as nominations. Equally countless were the visits he made to give support, advice and encouragement to the old, sick or distressed. One sometimes had the idea that he took a sort of mischievous delight in being a bit mysterious about this. For one of Bill's outstanding attributes was his sense of humour. Hearty bursts of laughter, quiet chuckles, wry jokes, and little pleasant surprises, made him a most agreeable companion, and lightened many a solemn occasion.

Another man significant in post-war Brighton Quaker life was Alan Staley (d.2005). A life-long pacifist like Bill Barber, he had appeared in 1939 before a CO tribunal. Raised a Methodist, he became a Quaker in 1945 and, as part of a reconciliation project worked in war-shattered Germany. He arrived in Brighton in October 1955 with his wife, Mary, and children Ruth and Paul. They were welcomed among Friends by Margaret Rundle, who later taught Ruth domestic science at Hove Girls' Grammar School. Alan Staley set up a Brighton peace group that later formed a nucleus of the Campaign for Nuclear Disarmament (CND). For forty years he was the convenor of the Brighton Friends Peace and Service Committee, which usually met in the meeting-house library, with its little gas fire providing great heat. An appropriate peace mural was once painted on the south side of the corridor from the meeting-house, showing Albert Schweitzer and others who worked for humanity and peace.

A Friend who came to Brighton Meeting in 1948 was Elizabeth Lees (née MacCallum). She was the daughter of Mabel MacCallum and the niece of Gladys Roberts, a powerful activist in the management of the Friends Centre. Mabel MacCallum was later remembered as a pretty lady with pink or bluey-white hair who had a 'foreign accent' – 'probably Scottish'! Elizabeth, then a solitary 16-year-old, remembers well the Staleys, Barbers and Devereuxs who were very kind to her. She remembers once doorkeeping for the meeting with an elderly woman Friend, letting in two latecomers. The older Friend was disapproving as the latecomers crept in and sat down: 'If they had an invitation to come and meet the King of England, they would have seen to it that they were on time, but it is only the King of Heaven whom they are hoping to meet here, so they don't care if they are late', she remarked with caustic, if misplaced, honesty.

One of the children attending Meeting in the 1950s was Melanie Barber. She recalls how Sunday was unfailingly taken up with the Meeting. One of the Elders overseeing this was William Marsh, who on entering through the Elder's door invariably checked the time of the meeting-house clock against his own pocket-watch, and was sufficiently tall to reach up to correct it if it was wrong. Other notable Elders were Walter Rowntree (1860-1957), with his trim white moustache and silver-topped stick, and Ronald Littleboy (1888-1965), who had married the niece of Maude Robinson. Ministry Melanie Barber still treasures was given by Ronald Littleboy, who used to quote from George VI's memorable war-time Christmas broadcast, 'I said to the man who stood at the Gate of the Year, "Give me a light that I may tread safely into the unknown", and he replied, "Go out into the darkness, and put your hand into the Hand of God. That shall be better than light and safer than a known way."'

Walter Rowntree, perhaps, left the greatest impression on Melanie Barber, 'as one of the first of many Friends that father ferried to and from the Meeting over the years':

On the way home he used to launch into reminiscing as soon as he had told us the number of Friends in Meeting that morning (usually seventy to eighty). He had, among other things, been a friend of [the Quaker politician] John Bright, to whom his mother had been house-keeper for the last few years of his life. As an inspired teacher and lec-turer Walter Rowntree often ministered in meeting, just before the children went out … and sometimes taking as his theme the beauty of the flowers on the table. The meeting held a ninetieth birthday party for him in 1950, in the lecture room, presenting him with flowers and a cake glowing with candles. He looked forward joyfully to reaching a century (he always checked the obituaries in the The Friend to see which of his Friends he had outlived) but died in hospital the day after his 97th birthday. The memorial meeting held in the meeting-house bedecked with flowers, saw Friends from far afield, including his contemporary, Barrow Cadbury, who despite his age, insisted on walking to the station.

This was Melanie Barber's first introduction to a memorial meeting and 'perhaps, one of the most inspired, bearing a real testimony to the grace of God in the life of this Friend.'

Barbara Barber's first visit to Brighton Meeting was in 1958, when she attended a weekend gathering of some 15 Sussex & Surrey Young Friends. Like many Friends she particularly remembered the traditional arrangement of wooden benches facing the Elder's bench under its acoustic sounding board. There were bare floorboards and the meeting commenced at 11 o'clock. Barbara and Barry Barber, the son of Gladys and William Barber, were married in the meeting-house on 10 January 1959. The meeting itself, in the 1950s, was quite an elderly meeting with only three or four children, and the social highlight of the year was the annual garden party at William and Margaret Marsh's home on the Ditchling Road.

During the 1950s and beyond, there was a surprising amount of acting talent within Brighton Meeting. Joan Crooke and her husband Keith, an attender, had been professional actors. Their daughter, Amaryllis, now of Worthing Meeting, is an actress. The radio actor John Ruddock was also a member of the Meeting, and Ellie Sedgwick, daughter of the meeting-house warden Margery Sedgwick, grew up to become a drama teacher. Rita Serjeant wrote several children's plays, which she also produced, including one with custom-written parts for many of the actors. Ruth Bahri (née Staley) remembers when the children mimed a reading of the parable of the sheep and the goats. In 1963, the Meeting's teenagers declared they wanted to produce their own play. Friends probably shook their heads over the choice of 'Archibald', a one-act play rather like a TV sitcom with confusion over identities and people deceiving each other. Although the comedy had little in the way of a message, everyone who participated learned a lot about responsibility, teamwork and loyalty.

The young Friends sometimes felt in awe of the Elders and Overseers who then still sat on the facing benches on the platform in front of the meeting. Among the youngsters attending meeting in those days were Melanie and Andre Barber, Ian and Stephen Pirie, Ellie Sedgwick, Ruth and Paul Staley, Ian Haydock, Isobel and Charles Crooke and others. Amaryllis Gunn (née Crooke) was very pleased when, as an adult, as is the practice, she was asked if she would like to confirm her membership, and then looked forward to staying in the meeting for worship for the whole period of time. Quaker meetings sometimes attract hangers on, and Brighton Meeting, like others, was blessed with a wide range of characters in addition to those attracted by the Friends Centre.

One attender at meetings was Reginald Davidson, a blind man (visually impaired, is today's euphemism). He always had a dog … golden labrador. This friend would minister regularly and at some length and at times just before our long fifteen minutes [of children's attendance] were up. I can remember our silent groans to this day. Actually, we were never convinced he was blind. He just had dark glasses – or was it a patch – to scare us. I mean, he always knew where his seat, his dog, us children were!

Gladys Barber, Mildred Whiting and Joan Crooke used to arrive at Meeting in the most glorious coloured clothes and Amaryllis Gunn remembers clearly how they lifted hearts – the colours and the personalities! Mildred once went shopping in one of the 'new-fangled supermarkets'. She left the shop and was wandering down the street when she realised she had not paid but still had the wire basket on her arm. Dashing back, she apologised profusely for her lack of memory. From behind, a woman announced, 'You can't doubt her word. She's a Quaker and they always tell the truth!' What a reputation earned by those before us, for us to live up to!

Gladys Barber lived to be Brighton Meeting's oldest member, and her benevolent influences still endure. She was wife, mother, grandmother, great-grandmother, peace activist, businesswoman, artist, needlewoman and much more. She supported every aspect of the Meeting. Her service included Children's Committee, Catering Committee, Peace Committee, Monthly Meeting Teenage Group, Meeting for Sufferings (the ongoing administration of the Yearly Meeting), Elders and Overseers. She was unstinting in her devotion to the commitments she took on. The Quarterly Meetings and Monthly Meetings once covered much wider areas, and she had many Friends in them. When Monthly Meeting was restructured into two – Lewes and Chichester – she missed the wider gatherings the original Monthly Meeting had provided. Gladys took much pleasure in the company of children, both hers and others. As well as four children she had ten grandchildren and five great-grandchildren.

Frank Norman and Pat Norman (née Cummins), who for thirty years from 1954 was secretary of the Friends Centre, joined Quakers in 1963 on their marriage. Frank Norman came of Quaker stock and, when a boy, had attended the Blue Idol meeting-house and a small nearby Quaker junior school. The running of the Friends Centre was not always an easy job for those involved in it, but the creative service and support and inspiration of so many Friends on its committees helped weather some difficult times. Also in 1963, the present writer was admitted as a member of Lewes and Chichester Monthly Meeting and still has the blue-bound book of Christian Faith and Practice given to him then by Deryck Hill, the Monthly Meeting Clerk, and with a label inscribed in the 'Plain Language' – 'Tenth-month 1963'.

I used to travel into town by train and this meant that I was often the first at the meeting-house. As I walked down from the railway station I would hear the bells from the different places of worship round about. For me, if not for George Fox, the sound was of infinite delight, a prayer going on all around me until I would begin to run for the sheer pleasure of hearing them. At the meeting-house I would distribute the hassocks or kneelers and leave a Bible on every bench or an introductory leaflet, 'Your First Time at a Quaker Meeting', for visitors. I felt as if I was preparing the stage for a great drama in which we would all participate as 'Our Heavenly Father' sought us in the silence and through the words of the ministry. In the meeting was the very smell of holiness and piety. It was not just polish or perfume but it clung to the very pages of the Bibles themselves and was more precious than incense to me.

One ancient Friend, Margaret Marsh, was very impressive. She was an Elder and sat up with a number of the other Elders and Overseers in the front of the meeting in their own little gallery. I used to like her messages, which she gave in a gentle and quavery voice like music. 'The healing of His seamless dress is by our beds of pain. We touch him in life's throng and press and we are whole again.' Her messages were often from the writings of the poet John Whittier. She used to glow with an inward peace and her gold spectacles would gleam. Once she asked me to sit next to her and shake hands with her to sig-nifiy the close of the meeting when the appropriate time came. I did not like sitting up in front of everyone! If I ever visited the meeting-house mid-week I would often see her getting ready to conduct a prayer meeting with hymns for elderly ladies. Such mid-week meet-ings hearkened back to a tradition only then dying out. There was also a First-day evening meeting for worship with a speaker, and a period of worship followed by discussion and a cup of tea. Some very strange Brighton characters used to appear at these – apart from myself!

Practical ecumenism had long been a keyword for Quakers but a new impetus for interchurch understanding came from Pope John whose encycli-cal 'Pacem in Terris' was studied by the Peace and Service Committee. Another issue that exercised the wider London Yearly Meeting was in 1963, when a group of Friends issued a pamphlet called 'Towards a Quaker View of Sex'. This discussed the sometimes unpalatable and suppressed facts of human sexuality that had caused secret suffering for many. It played a part in initiating a more open approach and, if it proved challenging to many traditionally minded people among Friends and others, did contribute to the changing attitudes of society at large.

These were also the days of peace activism often expressed through the CND, and one year many members of the Meeting staged a vigil at the Peace Statue at the boundary between Brighton and Hove. During the fiftieth anniversary of the ending of World War I an anthology of writings was presented and many Friends were involved. Amaryllis Gunn recalls it as an unbelievably moving experience, 'so much so that I can recall faces, feelings, even some of the poetry and prose. We all have special moments, like we have special books, special pieces of music. I can honestly say that that anthology for me was one of those, and had a remarkable influence on me.' The Peace and Service Committee had such an extended programme that a list of its activities in 1966 filled a typewritten foolscap sheet 'without any padding'.

The meeting-house was made available to local Muslims and their Imam before they had a mosque, and then, before the Friday prayers, queues of the devout would wait to go into the men's room for the ritual washing of feet. The meeting-house was also used on at least two occasions for Hindu weddings, when the Elder's bench was hung with the bride's dowry of colourful saris, with a ceremonial fire kindled and a canopy in the centre of the floor. Following the war the black-out blinds were removed and replaced by heavy velvet curtains. Danny, the Friends Centre caretaker, used to risk life and limb to take them down to beat with a Victorian carpet-beater, since dry-cleaning was so prohibitive in cost. Outside, the garden with its fig tree has been much appreciated by Brighton residents, and is seen in good weather as a precious oasis of calm in the town centre.

Over the years the meeting-house itself has not changed a lot in its purpose – as a building designed for meetings for worship, which are shorter now than once upon a time. The panelling, which was originally installed by Ron Nanscawen, is still there, but the old coke-hungry boiler has been replaced by central-heating. The coconut runners leading in from the entrance doors have gone, and so have the bare wooden floorboards, and where there used to be only benches for sitting on, Friends now have plastic chairs. So they have comparative luxury compared with their forebears. Pat Norman repaired the meeting-house cushions and Jessie Dicks repaired the runners for its remaining benches, and in 1981 a community embroidery project was started to make a nation-wide Quaker tapestry. The plan was to draw strength and inspiration from the past and to affirm faith in the future. Margaret Rundle was a great enthusiast for this, but there were few in Brighton with the necessary embroidery skills, so the Meeting worked with Friends in Worthing and Lewes to produce a panel.

Changes in Brighton Meeting also started to occur in the mid-1980s, when younger members with children started attending, building up a thriving Children's Meeting. And 'four or five years ago' some Friends felt encouraged to start an early First-day meeting because the main meeting had grown so big; the old tradition of mid-week meeting for worship has also been revived. As has become the practice in many Quaker meetings the Elder's bench, once seen as a visible embodiment of the meeting's authority and leadership, had fallen into disuse; now the new generation of Elders have ceased to sit visibly 'at the head of the meeting'. An additional 'Open Meeting' was also instituted to provide a forum for discussion of the meeting for worship that had preceded it. This was felt by some as 'not being in right ordering' and detracting from a proper reverence and attentiveness, but such discussion has, anyway, now become a part of Brighton's modern Quaker tradition.

Irrespective of physical and administrative changes, the spiritual atmosphere of the meeting-house has been maintained and, it is hoped, enhanced. Many people comment on the feeling they have of it as a place peaceful and welcoming. But there are all sorts of other surviving subtle and enduring influences contributed by many worthy seeking Friends, both past and present. As Brighton Meeting moves into the next 200 years of its meeting-house, it is well to remember that central to the activism of all the Friends past was that core and spiritual motivation without which all activity is vain. In a world so full of terror and catastrophe we may yet walk forward with hope and love 'into the unknown darkness' and know that in the hand of God will be found 'a way safer than light or any known way'.

Brief List Of Sources Consulted

The Records of the Religious Society of Friends for Lewes Monthly Meeting and Brighton Preparative Meeting held at the East Sussex Records Office, Lewes.

Abstracts of births, marriages and deaths held at Ship Street, Brighton.

David M. Butler, *Quaker Meeting Houses of Britain* (1999).

C.E. Clayton, 'Some Notes on the History of John Grover ...' in *Sussex Archaeological Collections*, Vol. 35.

J. Farrant, 'Sussex Schools' in *Sussex Archaeological Collections*, Vol. 122.

Edmund M. Gilbert, *Brighton: Old Ocean's Bauble* (1954; 2nd edn 1975).

Barbara Gold Harrison, 'An Anecdote relating to William Harrison of Brighton' in *Journal of the Friends Historical Society*, Vol. 10 (1913).

Percival Lucas, 'Some Notes on the Early Sussex Quaker Registers' in *Sussex Archaeological Collections*, Vol. 55.

Maude Robinson, 'Gleanings from the Minute Books of the Quarterly Meeting of Sussex' in *Journal of the Friends Historical Society*, Vol. 21 (1927).

——- 'A Girl's School at Lewes 100 Years Ago' in *Sussex County Magazine*, Vol. 8 (1934).

——- 'A Friends Meeting Eighty Years Ago' in *Friends Quarterly Examiner* (1946).

——— *A Southdown Farm in the Sixties* (1938, 2nd edn.1947).